Preschool in the Suzuki Spirit

Preschool
in the
Suzuki
Spirit

by Susan Grilli
foreword by Shin'ichi Suzuki

Harcourt Brace Jovanovich Japan
Tokyo, Japan

PHOTO CREDITS. Cover photographs, front and back, by Terry Buchalter and (back cover, upper left) Irene Laleuf. Photographers listed below in alphabetical order; numbers refer to pages on which photos appear.

John Flattau: 52 (top), 64, 137
Peter Grilli: 61
Osamu Honda: 140-41
Jill Krementz: 49, 55, 60, 144
Irene Laleuf: 50 (bottom left), 54, 63 (bottom)
Carmela McMahon: 63 (top), 132, 136 (bottom left)
Suzanne Opton: 52 (bottom), 58
Alan Perlman: 50-51 (top left and right), 53 (left),
    56-57, 59 (left), 62, 129, 130-131, 134-35
Mary Struthers: 143 (bottom)
TBS/TV Tokyo: 53 (right), 136 (top left)
Tanya Tesone: 59 (right)

First edition, 1987

Requests for permission to make copies of any part of the work should be addressed to: Harcourt Brace Jovanovich Japan, Inc., Ichibancho Central Building, 221 Ichibancho, Chiyoda-ku, Tokyo 102, Japan.

ISBN 0-15-673830-9

Designed by Dana Levy. Printed in Japan.

Publication Data:

Grilli, Susan, 1941–
Preschool in the Suzuki spirit.

1. Education—Preschool. 2. Education—in Suzuki method.
I. Title.

For Peter, with love

CONTENTS

FOREWORD

Man is a product of his environment. All over the world, children learn to speak the language of their native country. They develop a marvelous ability to speak it freely and effortlessly. Reflecting on the basis of this natural learning ability and the way in which it is acquired, I realized the following very important fact: Children learn their mother tongue by a method which is very different from the teaching methods practiced in today's elementary schools, where the curriculum moves quickly from one thing to the next. When children learn their mother tongue, ability is firmly and gradually developed at one level before advancing to the next. By this method, every child develops an excellent ability to speak his or her native language.

For example, when babies master three or four words, mothers encourage them to use those words every day as they talk to them. In the process of repeating those words, children gradually acquire the ability to speak. As their ability develops, they then add a few more words to their repertoire. As they repeat the words they know every day, their ability develops and deepens, and almost unnoticed, ten words grow to fifteen and they begin to speak. Adding words in this manner, their vocabulary increases in accord with their ability as they practice speaking every day, and they soon freely use many different words. By the time children are five or six years old, they have developed the ability to speak three or four thousand words—a fact which merits amazed admiration. This is none other than the result of training based on incremental practice. Here we have the secret of an educational method by which all children can develop their natural ability to an extraordinary degree.

Twenty-odd years ago, when I introduced the method abroad, it was widely appreciated. Known today as the Suzuki Method, more than three million children in over twenty countries have grown up studying violin and piano by this approach. It has been recognized as a revolution in education.

To return to the beginning of the discussion, since I knew that the mother-tongue method produced excellent results in teaching music, thirty-seven years ago I tried to find someone who would apply this method to teaching such subjects as mathematics and the Japanese language in elementary schools. Fortunately, I was able to arrange an important and highly successful experimental class at Hongo Elementary School in Matsumoto, Japan. In that class I saw that every student was successful in developing their natural abilities. When given the confidence that they can do things, children become cheerful and enthusiastic.

I thought this way of education should start before elementary school. Following my philosophy and this valuable experience, our Talent Education Pre-school was established here in Matsumoto. Not only Japanese but also many foreigners have been interested in our preschool and have visited here to observe our school and its activities and my philosophy has been introduced to the world.

I was glad to hear that The Suzuki Pre-School was started by Mrs. Susan Grilli in New York, and I have encouraged her to apply our Suzuki Method for very young children beyond music for these past twelve years. Now it's my great pleasure that Mrs. Grilli's book about her school has been published and her wonderful work and remarkable success will be shared with a large number of people, not only Suzuki Method teachers but also educators in general and all the parents of the world.

One of humanity's greatest blindnesses has been not realizing the excellent potential all children possess for developing superior abilities. Only children's native language is developed to a high level; in the world of what passes for education, a mistaken environment is created in which it is impossible for children to develop. Then it is said helplessly that the result is an outcome of children's innate superiority or inferiority.

Ability is not inborn. How thoughtless humans have been. Think of the present situation of the world's children in this inhospitable environment: although born with the wonderful gift of the life force, they are blighted by being raised in miserable circumstances. Sometimes, alone at night, I weep for them. How unkind this world is to its children! Let's seek the best way to highly develop every child!

I sincerely appreciate Mrs. Susan Grilli's time and great effort for young children's happiness, and I hope that more and more people will be able to understand our Suzuki movement and philosophy through her book.

Shinichi Suzuki

President & Director
Talent Education Institute

P R E F A C E

America is facing a real crisis in education. Children pass through our schools and emerge still uneducated. As graduates they are sadly unprepared for a society both technologically complex and morally uncertain, which fast seems to be running out of control. At this time, when the most preparation might not be enough, we let children slide through with little more than the least. And they know they are unprepared. They pay for this in personal problems that sometimes pervade the rest of their lives, and the lives of those around them.

My experience in preschool education has convinced me that this is unnecessary. We are being lax where we need to be vigilant. We are lowering our standards when we need to raise them. Children who have been undereducated pay the price in underachievement and moral confusion, and the society they enter does likewise. An awareness of inadequacy, which has its roots in an inadequate education, especially in the early years, lies just beneath the surface of many grown-up people. It is really not their fault that they are, truly, impaired: our schools themselves encourage diminished expectations and low levels of achievement.

I have seen two-and-one-half- to four-year-old children

achieve in The Suzuki Pre-School at a level beyond what was later asked of them in primary schools. When those schools clearly expected less of those children (and their parents), the children succumbed to this lack of stimulation and forgot their excitement for learning and for trying something new. This message—that education is something you drag yourself through, exerting minimal effort to meet minimal expectations, and that its goal is to be passed on to the next level, ready or not—is not the one we should be sending.

There are many social problems that we as Americans face. The low standard of literacy in this very affluent nation is the most shocking, followed by juvenile delinquency, which afflicts children who have not learned to do anything very well and who feel no special attachment to their society. The state of the American educational system has been recognized and articulated by many public figures. The governor of the state of New York, Mario Cuomo, is actively encouraging instruction in values in our schools, and in a recent keynote address at Harvard's three hundred fiftieth birthday celebration, Prince Charles of Great Britain warned that it has never been more important "to recognize the imbalance that has seeped into our lives and deprived us of a sense of meaning, because the emphasis has been too one-sided and has concentrated on the development of the intellect to the detriment of the spirit." Our own secretary of education, William J. Bennett, has released an eighty-three-page report called *First Lessons,* in which he writes: "The single best way to improve elementary education is to strengthen parents' role in it, both by reinforcing their relationship with the school and by helping and encouraging them in their own critical job of teaching the young."

It is time our national priorities were reversed; rather than spending most of our resources on the upper levels of a child's education, we must refocus on the earliest education given our children. Even though the years from birth to six are by now widely regarded as the most crucial for a child's entire later development, as a nation we underrate early childhood education appallingly. Those are clearly the years when we need to marshal our most intensive and creative educational forces.

This book is about one unique kind of preschool, which I think has applications and meanings far beyond its own walls.

The Suzuki approach to teaching very young children, with its belief in their great potential and its concern for them as sensitive, compassionate, and thoughtful as well as accomplished human beings, has much to give the world of education at large. Its concern that children find the best and the most authentic in themselves is one answer to many of the worries expressed in recent studies of the state of the U.S. educational system. Research spanning two decades in the Perry Pre-School Project in Ypsilanti, Michigan, points to what seems only logical: that children who have a better early start do better throughout their schooling and in their later lives as well. Rather than spending more and more of our resources correcting early mistakes or devising social solutions for the lack of the values and strengths that should be cultivated in childhood, we would do well to bring, in a newly strengthened partnership between parents and teachers, "a Suzuki feeling" to all early childhood education.

Our society can only benefit if its children get off to the right start. People *want* to be proud of what they know and can do well. The time is ripe for a strong swing in this direction, as the highly critical recent studies have shown, and it is not too late.

I present this book as a record of an experiment in early education that represents the possible. The excitement of our school is something I have experienced personally, through the vitality and accomplishment of the children in it. The Suzuki Pre-School is one example of putting the focus where I think it belongs, on earliest education. I don't pretend to have found *the answer,* the perfect environment for all young children. But since the foundations are laid in earliest childhood for the kind of standards one holds for the rest of one's life, the focus should rightly be on teaching *well* the first time around rather than depending upon remedial work, which is as costly in human as it is in economic terms. It is my hope that my own experience can provide inspiration and stimulate other similar experiments. It is a matter of national survival that we retain the strength we have as a nation by getting our priorities straight with regard to our most important resource, our children.

This book was written over a period of ten years, large parts of it appearing as articles and in the form of academic papers.

Speeches given at Suzuki conferences are a part of it as well. Some sections were developed specifically with teacher training in mind and some for the purpose of bringing Suzuki ideas to a wider audience than the Suzuki teaching world alone. It was not intended to be a curriculum in the strict sense, but rather an impression of the special spirit and feeling of a school. To me the ideas in this book reach beyond early education and affect us all as we face the uncertain future which is the inheritance of our children.

The reader will not find here a step-by-step "how-to" or a one-to-ten set of directions to be followed in a classroom. It seems to me that such a book would too severely limit the potential in each reader for personal creative development. My hope is that this book will largely serve as an inspiration for efforts in and out of the classroom for children in any environment.

A book like this and the school it reflects can never be considered the work of just one person. It is the product of the input of ideas from so many different directions and so many different people that it is impossible to list them all. Any teacher must be a sponge, soaking up good ideas from whatever sources are at hand. I would like to express my deepest appreciation to the following people, whose inspiration and faith in me made this book possible:

Shin'ichi Suzuki, without whose beautiful spirit and unquestioning faith in children's endless potential for happiness and success The Suzuki Pre-School would never have come to be. The many hours he spent with me sharing his ideas and the exciting work of his Talent Education Institute in Matsumoto, Japan, will always be deeply treasured. The children, parents, and teachers of The Suzuki Pre-School dedicate their work to their beloved friend and teacher, Shin'ichi Suzuki.

Waltraud Suzuki, for her warm friendship and special interest in me and my work.

Sylvia Edmunds, without whom my entire teaching career might never have happened. A superb teacher of teachers and of children, she has understood the Suzuki spirit better than anyone I have ever known. She is what every teacher needs: a fine mentor.

John Kendall, Elizabeth Mills, and Kay Slone—all early supporters of our school. Their broader vision of the Suzuki philosophy as more than music has again and again given me the affirmation

I needed to continue with something new in the Suzuki teaching world.

The Suzuki Association of the Americas, for all its encouragement as we prepared to begin a new chapter in teacher training.

Robert Reinsager, editor of the *American Suzuki Journal,* for helping me to use this excellent magazine as a first forum for my ideas.

Lucy Burrows of Bank Street College of Education, who was always so much more than an advisor had to be as I prepared the master's thesis on which this book is based. Her sensitive understanding and encouragement made me want to pursue this exciting experiment as far as it would go.

Tane Matsukata, founder and former headmistress of Nishimachi International School in Tokyo, Japan, who gave me my first opportunity to extend the Suzuki idea beyond music in her kindergarten. It was at Nishimachi that the Pre-School was really born.

All the teachers who have helped me develop The Suzuki Pre-School—especially Margot Cohn, Nancy Dexter, and Marai Yaw—each of whom has left her special and creative mark on the school.

Jeffrey Hunter, my editor, who has been of great help in shaping many disparate articles, academic papers, and speeches into a cohesive and readable book. His unusual sensitivity to me as a teacher and a writer has made our collaboration on this project a very special experience for me.

Kyoko Selden, who combines a special devotion to Dr. Suzuki and a sensibility as a translator with a uniquely warm perception of what my school is all about. She has thoughtfully preserved both the words and the spirit of this book for the Japanese reader.

Dana Levy, who has made the book beautiful to look at and who, for the sake of our friendship, took on this project on an impossibly tight schedule. His extraordinary eye for good design is a great gift to my book.

Anne Papantonio, vice-president of HBJ/New York, who first read the manuscript and whose invaluable suggestions vastly improved the book's chances for publication.

I am deeply indebted to the now more than one hundred and fifty families who have been a part of The Suzuki Pre-School through these first dozen years—to the children who helped us grow as people, and the parents who helped us teach, so often becoming excellent teachers themselves. Without their faith in us, this experiment in early education would never have flourished.

I owe much to the example set by my parents. Their perseverance, with compassion and humor, in search of quality in life, has proven to be the single most important element for me in pursuit of this marvelous yet challenging educational adventure.

My husband Peter has been my most thoughtful critic and most enthusiastic supporter through all these years of teaching and writing. His special awareness of the importance of this project, talent as an editor, and unique sensitivity to Japan have made it possible for me to keep my enthusiasm for the project high and explore a good deal more of my own potential, Suzuki style, than I ever thought possible.·

OUR BEGINNINGS, OUR GOALS

N othing in my life had quite prepared me for the sounds I heard from Sylvia Edmunds' tape recorder that foggy summer morning in 1967. She swore the Vivaldi concerto I was hearing was being played by five- and six-year-old children, but I simply did not believe her. Then she switched off the machine and opened a tiny violin case, handing me the instrument inside. My hands were all clammy as I lifted it up to my chin—was I to audition for the job on this one-eighth-sized violin? Sylvia laughed and said, "That one's a big one—you should see the one-sixteenths!"

Relaxed now and feeling freer about this whole interview, I inspected the tiny violin more closely. It was nearer in quality to my full-sized instrument than I would have guessed it could be. Much of this instrument was hand crafted, its varnish was a beautiful color, and it had a surprisingly good tone for so small a box. Clearly, this was no toy. I began to try to imagine a group of small children playing Vivaldi on such instruments—and that was what I would hear a month later at my first Suzuki concert. If I was impressed and disbelieving at the interview, I was overwhelmed at the concert. Ten children aged six to seventeen, touring from

Japan, walked through the audience playing the first movement of Vivaldi's A Minor Concerto, with such strong technique, beautiful tone, and sensitive interpretation that many members of the audience were in tears. The children took their places on the stage without missing a beat and bowed politely when they were finished. I felt I would never be quite the same again after experiencing such a moving and professional performance from children so young. How had they accomplished so much, and with such feeling? The speed of their fingers, richness of their tone, and their self-assurance were absolutely mind-boggling. Yet when the children were not playing, they behaved just like normal happy children anywhere, laughing and playing with their American hosts after the concert.

In Harwich, Massachusetts, where Sylvia and I had begun our teaching together at the public elementary school (Sylvia had won a Title III grant for experiments in creative education), I had seen a film that prepared me somewhat for the astonishing musical accomplishments of these children. It showed Pablo Casals rushing up to the stage after a concert by Suzuki students in Tokyo. Overcome by emotion as he embraced Dr. Suzuki, Casals had exclaimed, "Perhaps this is music that will save the world!"

Sylvia, a "natural" as a Suzuki teacher, made me believe I could do anything I wanted to. I was determined to do my very best for her and for the children we would teach together. She suggested that our challenge would be to develop a whole new curriculum, tailoring the Suzuki method to the needs of the children of Harwich in their public school setting. Believing each teacher must develop her own personal style, she advocated taking inspiration from Dr. Suzuki and then transforming his method into one's own, always keeping in mind that it was up to teachers and parents to make sure children were successful.

My experience with this fine teacher who brought out the best in me, Suzuki style, was rich in experimentation and innovation. We felt free to bounce ideas off one another, to give the children the best curriculum we could devise, and always keep it as fun and lively as possible. We felt very comfortable together, and I believe we complemented each other well and learned as much from our mistakes as from our successes. It was the complex of qualities in this experience, including Sylvia's personal example and the way she guided an inexperienced teacher like me, that I came to recognize as "the Suzuki feeling."

Then came the day a kindergartner said to me, "I hate school, but I *love* the violin!" That child was expecting me to be pleased with the "love the violin" part, but instead, I was curious and worried about "I hate school." Putting my ear shamelessly to the wall of the kindergarten classroom one day, I found out the reason for his feelings, as I overheard the following exchange between teacher and student:

Teacher: "Isn't that a black house?"
Small Voice: "Yes."
Teacher: "Have you ever seen a black house?"
Smaller Voice: "No."
Teacher: "Well, there is no such thing as a black house. I don't ever want to see you painting a house black again!"
No Voice at All: " . . . "

This one-sided "exchange" between a student and his overwhelmingly powerful teacher, who had successfully cowed him as she had many others, was probably the single most important inspiration for my own school, albeit a negative one. Children would *not* hate school if I could help it. Why not bring the Suzuki method, which had led that one child to love the violin, to the whole curriculum? Why patronize children in other areas of early learning, when they had shown how happy they were through their successes with the Suzuki approach to music?

It was not until 1971, when I was living in Japan, that I was given the opportunity I needed to try out some of my own ideas. Deeply impressed by the work of Dr. Suzuki's experimental kindergarten in Matsumoto, Nagano Prefecture, I began to dream of incorporating some of these innovations into a regular kindergarten curriculum. A remarkable Japanese woman named Tane Matsukata was to give me my first chance. She is the founder of the Nishimachi International School and a strong-minded educational innovator in her own right. She liked my ideas and decided to take a chance on me. Refusing to let my lack of education-school degrees stand in the way, she hired me to teach her kindergarten. Feeling my way through that year at Nishimachi, experimenting throughout the full range of a kindergarten curriculum by injecting a "Suzuki feeling" into it whenever possible, I found results exciting beyond my greatest expectations. Dr. Suzuki's ideas translated very well indeed into projects in science, art, language, and math; these ideas could be expressed much more broadly, it turned out, than through music alone. And the children followed their teacher's lead—if she assumed they had no limitations, they assumed the same thing. Although I loved teaching kindergarten, I began to envision developing a similar curriculum for the preschool level, working with even younger children and catching them when they were most open to the world around them. If Dr. Suzuki could successfully teach violin to children of two and one-half, why not teach other areas of early learning in the same positive and productive way?

Back in the United States, I joined the faculty of School for Strings, a Suzuki violin school in New York City founded and directed by Louise Behrend. There I met Margot Cohn and Nancy Dexter who, independently, shared many of my feelings about early education. We agreed that violin lessons for very young children, isolated from their other schooling, seemed unnatural; they should be incorporated and integrated into a full range of other learning activities. With Louise Behrend's encouragement, the three of us began what is now called The Suzuki Pre-School. The school opened on October 3, 1974, with ten students and three teachers—a most luxurious ratio of adults to children! We had an exciting first year and learned a great deal, day by day, about how to run a nursery school.

Feeling the need to expose our children to a broader educational setting, we sought to combine the school with one that would offer more diverse learning experiences for a wider age group. This we believed would serve as the inspiration our children needed but were now getting only through music. (At School for Strings much fine practicing and many a concert could be heard, but equal stimulation was needed in other areas, too, if our school was to do for children what it had set out to do.) We joined Manhattan's The Day School in 1975. In 1976, headmaster Tom Mansfield, wanting to bring Suzuki ideas into the curriculum, put us in charge of his Nursery. This experience was invaluable in giving us the training and courage necessary to strike off on our own. In 1978, we became an independent non-profit organization, responsible for our own future. Our excitement outweighed any apprehensions we had as we arranged to rent space at New York's Cathedral of St. John the Divine. The Cathedral leadership, particularly Dean James Parks Morton, saw the Pre-School imaginatively as a microcosm of all the stimulating activities of this innovative center of Manhattan culture. There our children were exposed to the sounds of Richard Westenburg's Musica Sacra chorus rehearsing an oratorio with full orchestra, the classes at the Big Apple Circus school, and the friendship of four resident peacocks—Matthew, Mark, Luke, and Joan(!)—whom the children loved meeting in full plumage as we explored the thirteen glorious acres of that unique oasis in the middle of an otherwise crowded and uncompromising city.

Since 1981, The Suzuki Pre-School has found its most comfortable home as part of the Hastings Talent Education Center, a Suzuki music school started with teachers sent directly by Suzuki from Japan in the late 1960s. In a very special way we have come full circle, since one of our original founders, Nancy Dexter, directs Hastings Talent Education. In order to incorporate the Pre-School physically, the music school had to find a new home. An immaculately maintained church, the Aldersgate United Methodist, was found within one mile of the old location. Five large, cheerful, light, and airy rooms on four beautiful parklike acres were available for rent. We are fortunate to have the support and interest of Reverend Stuart Thody of Aldersgate. There is an unusually warm spirit of cooperation between church and school that positively influences the mood of the school, not only for students and teachers but for parents as well. The physical and psychological peacefulness of the place definitely affects the way we all learn together. And perhaps most important, the future of the preschoolers' music education can be assured, since Hastings Talent Education provides continuity in Suzuki violin instruction for Pre-School graduates.

Although adding Suzuki music lessons to a regular preschool is an interesting and worthwhile experiment, this is not what we are doing at The Suzuki Pre-School. We really try to approach each subject area, step by step, Suzuki style. Our school is approved by Dr. Suzuki and the Suzuki Association of the Americas for teacher training. We have given teachers' workshops for three years and this year will be training a teacher full-time, on the job.

We hope that many new Suzuki-based experiments in early education will spring up as a result of these attempts at dissemination. It is unfortunate that we cannot pick up our school and travel with it, that people have to make a trip to New York to see what we are doing. We plan to make many videotapes in the future to aid teachers in faraway places who are struggling with the exciting but challenging prospect of starting their own schools, for we know—only too well—that these teachers need every bit of help and encouragement they can get.

The Suzuki idea has far greater implications than its application through music alone, and it is exciting to see the growing recognition of this worldwide, and, especially, in Dr. Suzuki's lifetime. For us in the West it is important and useful to recognize that Dr. Suzuki's approach to learning is shared by many other innovative and thoughtful teachers and writers on education. Maria Montessori, Sybil Marshall, and Sylvia Ashton-Warner are only a few of those who agree strikingly with the thinking of Dr. Suzuki, and in the following chapter we will examine the Suzuki idea and Western proponents of similar approaches to education at greater length. (The bibliographies suggest a wide variety of further reading along these lines.) But in spite of the sympathetic chords struck on this side of the Pacific, we must realize that the situations in Japan and the United States are rather different. In Japan, where the literacy rate is almost at one hundred percent, every adult seems proud to command a basic set of facts about the world around him. To be sure, I often wish for more creative thinking to accompany those facts, but this basic education gives people an undeniable confidence, pleasure, and competence. What if we could combine that Japanese passion for facts and skills with Western ingenuity, creative thinking, and expressiveness? This is the dream of our Pre-School. Our aim is to find the best of our world for our children, wherever it can be found; to avoid being locked in to one approach, but instead to be open to the secrets of good learning however they might be discovered. More important than even philosophy or method is the *spirit* of Suzuki teaching—the inspiration to reach beyond oneself into the innermost recesses of creativity and imagination residing in each of us, that adults feel from watching Suzuki himself.

The reinvolvement of parents in children's learning is another of Suzuki's great contributions to our uncertain world. The only limitations on young children's learning, he insists, are those of the adults around them. We encourage adults working with children to become modern Renaissance people, as interested as their children in everything in the world around them and willing to learn about whatever they don't know for those children's sake. A cooperative teacher-parent effort to make adults richly responsive resources for children's learning dispels tensions between home and school and maximizes the possibility that children will maintain their natural and innate excitement about learning rather than tragically lose it when they go to school. Parents have many skills and interests to share with children. We teachers can show them how. And when our skills are not adequate, we can bring into the classroom talented adults from outside, to share their enthusiasm and abilities with the children; or we can bring older children into the classroom to become teachers of younger ones. Some of America's very best teaching seems to have taken place in one-room schools, and I can see why: the mixture of younger and older students can be astonishingly inspiring. The participation of parents and other talented adults in our Suzuki Pre-School is the subject of chapter 5.

Adapting the Suzuki method to preschool teaching is, of course, the core of this book. We present an exploration of both methods and materials. As in Suzuki violin teaching, the Pre-School first approaches each subject area through exposure. The child absorbs from a rich environment until he appears ready for actual instruction. Then we must be on the spot to teach, but only as much as the child is ready to learn. We build carefully, one learning step at a time. With truly careful preparation and an artfully entertaining style, a teacher can give a child a thoroughly solid foundation of skills, in an atmosphere of fun. Only through the experience of doing something really well can a child become truly creative. And given that experience, young children's attention spans can be stretched far beyond what is usually believed possible. If something is wonderfully absorbing and fascinating, a child will not want to give it up.

In all learning, children clearly can do much more than has previously been thought possible. If the atmosphere is right, the school almost seems to run itself, with children independently following their own unique interests, using teachers and parents only when they can't figure something out by themselves or with the help of another child. Teachers must closely observe children's individual learning patterns, paying careful attention to the stages of development they are passing through. Special thought must be given to creating an entirely separate curriculum for each child and revising it on a daily basis if what you observe of a child's progress requires it. You must be prepared to throw out all your most carefully laid plans for a child if he or she requires new ones. Chapter 4, which presents a case study of one child's development within our Suzuki Pre-School setting, offers a concrete example of the adaptability and sensitivity required of teachers in a school like ours.

The Suzuki Pre-School aims to build memory, quickness of thought, listening, concentration, sensitivity to others, and self-esteem. Games that develop sense awareness, alert response, and keen observation are central to all our work. We look for toys and books that grow with the children; we reject those that patronize them. We've learned to ignore manufacturers' and publishers' ideas of age-appropriateness. They are often based on the marketability of the product or book and seldom reflect the real needs of the children for whom they are intended. As P.L. Travers of *Mary Poppins* fame has said, "For every book is a message, and if children happen to receive it and like it, they will appropriate it to themselves no matter what the author may say or what label he gives himself."

Through analogies from the children's own experiences, we adapt all kinds of learning tools and ideas—often geared toward older children—to the needs of our students. The Pre-School probably offers children a greater number of projects that develop fine muscle coordination than are usually found in early childhood programs. The violin, far from a special subject separate from all others, becomes a regular part of the classroom, to be explored along with other subjects. It is because we teach the violin that we need to prepare children's fingers and hands to do more complex and subtle things, but it is also because we have noticed a lack of this fine muscle ability in general in adult Americans that we stress its importance. As the year progresses, projects in all areas grow more and more sophisticated and may well be suggested by advancing work on the violin: for example, a violin class may inspire a science project, such as trying out the effect of tuning forks in glasses of water. In aiming for an integration of all subject areas while keeping in mind the individual integrity of each, a story may lead to a math, art, or music project. Theater games can develop out of almost any activity, and you can make up a poem about just about anything. I have gathered many of these sample materials and exercises and included them in an appendix for the inspiration of those who wish to experiment with our approach. In some ways, they give the clearest picture of our teaching short of visiting the classroom. Because of the importance of music in our method, an appendix, Suggested Listening (for parents and children at home), has been included as well.

Of course no curriculum is the last word, the ultimate solution which will permit you to sit back and relax for the rest of your teaching career. We never have *the* answer, something that works every time for every child. The ideas in this book have grown out of the experiences of one small group of teachers in one small school. The more successful those ideas have been, the clearer it's seemed that the possibilities for variations on these themes are endless. We have learned, first, that it is up to each individual teacher to adapt the Suzuki method and make it her own, and that process—which is also an exciting human adventure—is what this book is about.

PART ONE

THE
SUZUKI
IDEA

I n order to insure that no child would ever again say to us "I hate school but I love the violin," we decided to try to bring the success and happiness of the Suzuki music method to all aspects of an early childhood classroom. At national and international Suzuki conventions and in our own workshops for teachers, it has become increasingly clear that interest in starting schools such as ours runs very high. We also find more and more Suzuki teachers broadening work in their music studios with preschool ideas. A recent and exciting development is that a number of early childhood teachers not trained in Suzuki techniques or even specifically in music have sought these ideas for use in their own classrooms. To me it seems clear that the reason for this gathering interest is because Dr. Suzuki's ideas are timeless and natural, making good sense wherever they are thoughtfully and sensitively applied, and classic in that they live through and beyond many an educational fad.

I have been asked, "Why is this idea of extending the Suzuki method beyond music so important?" To me the answer is clearly that the preschool, kindergarten, and maybe even eventually the primary school are the natural next steps to take, seeing how successful the Suzuki approach is in music. Dr. Suzuki thinks so too, and makes this expansion of his idea one of the most important world-wide aims of the newly developed International Suzuki Association. But for those new to Dr. Suzuki and his way of teaching, a brief presentation of his approach and his core ideas is necessary, and that is the purpose to which I have devoted this chapter.

All this talk of Dr. Suzuki's ideas may mislead the reader to expect that he is mainly an educational theorist. This couldn't be farther from the truth, as a moment in a class led by Dr. Suzuki would reveal. Watching Shin'ichi Suzuki teach small children is a delectable experience in observing a wise and child-like elf, in charmingly witty rapport with these children, whom he clearly loves. Show Suzuki a small child, and watch his eyes light up! You can see the mutual fascination developing between child and teacher, whatever the child's nationality. Suzuki fills the room where he is teaching with the magic of his personal energy and magnetism, moving light-footedly and light-heartedly through exciting, fast-paced classes. He is a true Pied Piper of the violin. Usually speaking in a charming mixture of English, Japanese, and German (as a young man he studied for eight years in the Berlin of the twenties with violinist Karl Klingler), Suzuki may say something about "bringing up the delicacy of the ear"—and you know perfectly well what he means. What's more, you work hard to understand every word, since the man is so fascinating. (Now eighty-eight, he's still meeting a full teaching, traveling, and lecturing schedule.) Suzuki can make children do *anything,* they adore him so. I think they see him as uniquely one of their own, perhaps a sort of E.T., in on the secrets of childhood as few adults are. Suzuki makes everyone around him feel newly energized. It is his special brilliance to be able to make people of all ages feel they could do just about anything. He seems to bring out the best in everybody.

Despite his light touch and the joking he does with children, which he often turns on himself ("Students better than teacher!"), there is always a very clear purpose behind Suzuki's pleasant, relaxed manner. He'll have in mind one specific teaching idea and will proceed brilliantly to display a logical progression of different ways to say this same thing until his student or students have a completely clear idea of what he wants and how to do it. And all of this takes place in a totally delightful atmosphere of fun and intimacy between students and teacher. He plans ever so carefully to be sure he has a child thoroughly prepared to do what he is asking. And he makes the child feel it is a wonderful accomplishment when he or she succeeds. The lesson stops just a little before children are ready to stop, so they'll be doubly eager for the next session together with him. He believes in children so wholeheartedly that they believe in themselves, and the music they produce under his direction is simply astounding.

An observer need not speak a word of Japanese to follow the general drift of lessons. Suzuki relies refreshingly on *showing* much more than explaining. (How many classrooms have we all tolerated where too much talk killed the subject for us forever?) When he does speak to the children, he most often uses analogies from their own experience that are calculated to make them smile and wake up their brains. The pace of his classes is quick and rhythmical. Few of us Suzuki teachers can keep up with the limber quickness of Suzuki himself. He seems made of rubber, his body is so relaxed. And when he works with children, he seems half his age. He jokes about retiring at the age of one hundred ten, yet nobody who knows him can possibly imagine him *ever* retiring. I recently visited him at Matsumoto and found him giving a class for teacher-trainees after delivering a speech at a nearby college—on a Sunday! Despite this heavy schedule, he made time for me, too—as he always has when I've visited him. My memories of all those visits are a priceless possession. Just thinking of them gives a shot in the arm to my own teaching whenever it begins to get a little humdrum and slow.

Suzuki's "mother-tongue method" is based on the way children learn their native language through exposure, example, repetition, and refinement. Suzuki notes that parents possess an instinctive approach to language teaching. Constant exposure and stimulation encourage young children to learn this skill at an astonishing rate. By the time children reach the age of four, they command several thousand words. Progress takes place at the child's own natural rate, and practice is a built-in and pleasurable part of daily learning. Suzuki's own summary of his philosophy, as expressed by John Kendall, one of this country's earliest and best Suzuki teachers, is based on the idea that the human being is the product of his own environment. (In fact Suzuki gives little heed to a person's inheritance, feeling that anyone can be taught if approached correctly.) Exposure to the best in our culture cannot start early enough in a child's life. Repetition of experiences, something young children naturally like, is important to all learning. Teachers and parents (the adult human environment) must both be of the highest possible level of quality and willing to continue intellectual growth throughout their lives, to provide a rich learning environment for the developing child. The attitude of the parents is seen as absolutely crucial. The teacher must thoroughly understand exactly what steps to take with the child, and when and how to take them. Dr. Suzuki says we are educating for *life* through the violin (or any other subject). He calls his movement Talent Education and his school the Talent Education Institute, since he believes all children are born with natural talent and that it is the responsibility of adults to develop it well. Suzuki aims to produce happy, well-educated children whose lives are as full of goodwill toward others and the constant search for what is most beautiful in the world as they are with the rewards of their own considerable accomplishments. He does not aim to produce professional violinists, but rather excellent amateur players who will always enjoy music as a central and civilizing part of their lives. Suzuki believes that ability breeds ability; once you've experienced doing something really well, you've gotten naturally into the habit of risking trying other new things, too. This is what he means by "the habit of action."

Suzuki feels it is important to expose children to the greatest people of their age, in all fields. As a young man studying in Germany, he had a great mentor of his own. Through Karl Klingler, his violin teacher, Suzuki was introduced to and greatly influenced by Dr. Albert Einstein and his special circle of friends. With the example of some of the most extraordinary people of his age before him, Suzuki came to feel he must try to stretch his own potential—and later, the potential of the children he taught—as far as it would go. In devastated postwar Japan, Suzuki wanted to do something to bring hope back to Japan's sadly demoralized children. He started with only one small violin, and he went from house to house teaching with it. Forty years later, he oversees thousands of Suzuki teaching centers all over the world and presides over an annual Tokyo concert of over three thousand children from all over Japan who play the music literature they have learned in common. Four principal instruments are represented: violin, piano, cello, and flute. Recent concerts have included exciting orchestra and chamber music work by children. These concerts are thrilling, but of greatest interest to me is the work of the experimental Kindergarten in Matsumoto and Early Development Association in Tokyo, which extend the Suzuki idea beyond music.

Though Dr. Suzuki's philosophy may be unfamiliar to many in early childhood education, there are many educational thinkers and innovators, perhaps better known in the West, whose ideas harmonize remarkably with his. They are obviously a great shorthand method for introducing the Suzuki idea without going into detail inappropriate to this book's purpose, which is more practical than theoretical. Keeping in mind six elements—exposure, imitation, encouragement, repetition, addition, and refinement—common to both children's first language learning and the Suzuki method of music instruction, I have collected the thoughts of a number of other great educators.

Jane Bland, author of *Art of the Young Child* and a teacher of art for young children at Bank Street College of Education, speaks of the parent as the child's first art teacher, a person whose job it is to encourage a superior environment. She also makes the same connection Suzuki does with the learning of language: "That child is lucky whose parents and teachers are as delighted with each forward step in the language of art, as they are with each new venture in speech."

In *Writing for Children,* Claudia Lewis finds the child by nature a close observer of the world, "tapping the world through feeling, touch, sight, and sound. Through rhythmic repetition he learns the complexities of language and is naturally interested in enumerating, recounting, contrasting, repeating, reviewing." The preschool child "stops for every blade of grass."

The Russian poet Kornei Chukovsky is fascinated by the child's vast mental effort to master his own language, that makes him the "hardest mental toiler on our planet." In a book bursting with excitement and faith in the enormous abilities of children,

From Two to Five, Chukovsky shows that children value knowledge above all else. Writing about language acquisition, he notes that imitation is the basis for aptitude (an idea that is the foundation for Suzuki's Talent Education). If a child speaks well, he will think well. Most important are the earliest songs and rhymes of the mother. Humor is a precious quality that enhances a child's perspective and tolerance. A wonderful storyteller himself, Chukovsky agrees with what we have seen in our classroom, that through storytelling we foster humanity and compassion in young children.

In *Music and Young Children,* Frances Aronoff shows how direct experiences in music lay the foundation for concept formation and skills in science, social studies, and language. The spontaneity and confidence generated by self-expression through music and movement is transformed to other learning challenges. Most interestingly, and very much in agreement with Suzuki, she says the idea of "musical talent" is a romantic mystique that intimidates lay persons. Talent is something that can be developed. (Too many people, it seems to me, have been told they aren't musically talented, and that, sadly, is often the end of any musical efforts on their part.) Aronoff quotes the educator Harold Taylor's remark that "in the young child we find a natural poet, natural musician, a person who is accustomed to responding to aesthetic values by his very nature."

The Uses of Enchantment is a wonderful affirmation of fairy tales for young children. In it child psychologist Bruno Bettelheim sounds just like Suzuki when he points out that if children are reared so that their lives are meaningful to them, they will not need special help. "Of the first importance . . . is the impact of parents and others who take care of the child; second is our cultural heritage, if it is transmitted to the child in the right manner."

Burton White, director of the Center for Parent Education in Newton, Massachusetts, notes that until now society has never assumed the responsibility of training prospective parents for one of their most difficult functions, their role as teachers. In the curriculum materials for an exciting educational experiment called BEEP (Brookline Early Education Project), he says, "We spend nothing on a child's most important years, when the foundations of his educational capacity are being set. Then we spend more and more, as he grows older, when he needs it less and less. . . . The newborn may be able to learn better in the first six months of life than ever again. . . . Not only the rate but the direction of the development may be determined by the environment that these early capacities have." One cannot help thinking of the title of Suzuki's book, *Ability Development from Age Zero.*

An important breakthrough in research on babies is documented in *Child Alive!* edited by Roger Lewin. Through the use of slow-motion photography, he and other researchers have discovered that newborn babies move to the rhythms of their mothers' speech. Later, when babies learn to speak, their bodies have been responding to the rhythms of that language for a long time, giving them an important kind of practice that is pre-speech. Babies have a built-in ability to seek out sound and try to follow it. When the mother is not interacting with the baby, the baby is withdrawn, even depressed. "If the intense innate curiosity of children in their early years is not exploited," remarks Lewin, "it may be wasted forever."

It is startling that men and women working at different times and in very different parts of the world can come to such similar conclusions about the development of young children. Suzuki has yet to attain the degree of recognition in educational circles that he rightly deserves. Perhaps it is because his brilliant contributions to knowledge about how children learn have come more through his teaching than through theoretical writing. The fact that he is working outside the Western world, in Japan, keeps him somewhat isolated from other educators, who may still wrongly harbor the feeling that what he is doing really only works with Japanese children. Finally, the medium of music in which he works is itself seen as a kind of specialty, a kind of "extra" subject in the world of general education. Actually, Suzuki would do what he does for children through *any* subject; he uses the violin simply because that is what he knòws best. Suzuki is indeed an extraordinary educational innovator, for what he does for small children has potential applications in every kind of early childhood classroom, in any country. The children know it, but the educational establishment is just a little bit slower at catching on.

In *All Our Children,* a study done for the Carnegie Corporation, Kenneth Kenniston concludes that schools have taken away the educational function from parents, and that there is a need for the reinvolvement of parents in children's learning. Since that report, Suzuki instruction has burgeoned in the U.S. This is no accident, since it meets that pressing national need for parents and children to work together, and meets it so superbly.

Suzuki teachers thinking of expanding their teaching to other areas of early learning as well as music seem to think first and foremost of Maria Montessori as the educational thinker most compatible with Suzuki. Though her writings certainly suggest this compatibility, many Montessori classrooms are rather rigid—parents have been strictly excluded and children put to work unimaginatively on what should be highly creative Montessori learning apparatus. I feel Montessori would be shocked at the relatively cold and uncompromising quality of some of what I have seen being done in her name. This is always the danger after the death of a great educator: that well-intentioned but unimaginative people will "lock in" and rigidify their ideas in an attempt to preserve them. It could happen to Suzuki, too—we must be sure it doesn't! In our school we use much Montessori-type equipment that we have made ourselves. It would have been wonderful if she and Suzuki could have known one another—both believe, as she says, that all spheres of human activity are made meaningful to the child through his successful mastery of any activity.

We have used *Workjobs* by Mary Baratta-Lorton in our classroom as a recipe book for making our own skill-building equipment, basically from inexpensive, scrounged materials. An exceptionally creative teacher, she feels that for far too many children school is a place to *stop* learning for the first time in their lives. A teacher, she says, must have a combination of thorough preparation and "derring-do." To over-explain is to kill a child's interest in the subject. Baratta-Lorton believes, just as Suzuki does, that the accumulated confidence and skill which a child gains by going one step at a time leads to clearer and more confident self-expression.

Robert Pirsig, in *Zen and the Art of Motorcycle Maintenance,* develops a complex and compelling argument for quality, which he spells with a capital *Q:* "You have to have a sense of what's good . . . this sense isn't just something you're born with. It's the direct result of contact with Quality." I have seen children in my class respond naturally to greatness in a performance by giving it their attention for an hour or more—children who are at an age level usually said to have an attention span of a mere ten minutes!

Sybil Marshall's *An Experiment in Education* is about a curriculum built in depth through many subject areas, around Beethoven's "Pastorale" Symphony—but about a great deal more as well. She sees children as "by nature motivated to learn when the learning situation is one of exploration and discovery—it is equally natural for them to want to practice skills of all kinds, until they have mastered them. . . . Children are geared toward growing up, their curiosity, ingenuity, creative ability and boundless energy are tools employed to obtain such experience."

It was from reading Alice Murton's *From Home to School* that I got the greatest encouragement for the "family grouping" of students of different ages that I wanted for the Pre-School. She sees parents and teachers as privileged to share in the development and progress of children: "The overall need, in schools for young children, is companionship of understanding adults of all ages and kinds, working in cooperation with the teacher, and ready to play their part in children's need to communicate, not only with their peers, but with adults of every age. . . . To separate children of three, four, and five in age groups [is] to deny the normal pattern of home life." Above all, we must be sure not to create a gap between home and school.

Dorothy Cohen, author of *The Learning Child,* takes this idea further when she sees the necessity of parents and teachers being allies if we are to succeed in "inculcating in children the open minds and warm hearts that, coupled with skills and information, will surely be of value to them" in a troubled world they must help to change. "It may be a matter of [children's] survival that we succeed."

A teacher whose work has been as great an inspiration to me as Suzuki's is Sylvia Ashton-Warner. Her lyrical book *Teacher* is at the top of any reading list I might make for teacher-trainees. She brings not only intelligence but real passion to teaching and describes her work in a deeply moving and articulate way. Working with Maori children in New Zealand, she is really saying the same thing as Suzuki working with Japanese children. Both are aiming for world peace through education: "The more the creative vent widens, the more the destructive one atrophies. . . . Wherever there's creativity on a large scale, there's life."

A startling study by Benjamin Bloom of the University of Chicago on the elements common to exceptional achievers cites the importance of the years between birth and five or six in terms of the development of intelligence and school achievement. "There is more growth during those years than during any equal number of years later in life." Saying that the ingredients necessary for such exceptional achievement in children include parents who themselves enjoy sports, music, and intellectual pursuits, Bloom notes parents must effectively convey those feelings to children and believe in the work ethic. These ingredients can be found in most successful Suzuki parents.

The New York Times of December 11, 1979 had an article by Gene Maeroff, "Special Education in Regular Classrooms," that encouraged us to continue an experiment we had begun. We had been using materials developed to reteach the basics to handicapped children with normal preschool children learning those skills for the first time. Maeroff records an increasing trend by experts to investigate the possibility that all students might benefit from instructional methods developed for the handicapped—a system of setting instructional objectives and then insuring that a student learns one set of skills before tackling the next (Suzuki's "one new idea at each lesson"). Also needed with normal children is the increased role of the parent, which is essential with the handicapped.

Dr. Reuben Feuerstein (in *The New York Times,* March 24, 1981, "Nature vs. Nurture: Israeli Psychologist Urges Active Intervention") comments that adults are not merely dispensers of information to children, but are mediators of learning experience: the adult explains or changes the stimuli on the child's behalf. The important thing is the adults' degree of caring and effort. Intelligence can be *taught,* he says, and should not be regarded as unchangeable. The teacher must look to himself if the child doesn't succeed. This is exactly what Dr. Suzuki believes and practices.

Since the study by the National Commission on Excellence in Education was released in April of 1983, with its somewhat grim conclusions about the general state of American education, much consciousness-raising has begun about attaching greater importance to schools and teachers, but we have a long way to go before our priorities are really straight. The report's major premise was that "The educational foundations of our country are presently being eroded by a rising tide of mediocrity that threatens our very future as a nation and a people." A more recent report, *A Nation Prepared: Teachers for the 21st Century* (by the Task Force on Teaching as a Profession, for the Carnegie Forum on Education and the Economy) appeared in May 1986. Its ambitious aims are set forth in the section called "Executive Summary": "In this new pursuit of excellence . . . success depends on achieving far more demanding educational standards than we have ever attempted to reach before, and . . . in creating a profession equal to the task—a profession of well-educated teachers prepared to assume new powers and responsibilities to redesign schools for the future."

In *The New York Times* of May 22, 1977, David Rockefeller Jr. ("Wanted: A New Policy for the Arts in Education") writes that there is "a crying need to expand the concept of literacy to include the language of gesture (theater), image (the visual arts), sound (music), movement (dance), and space (architecture). Extraordinary powers of discrimination are required to guide us through the buzzing confusion of contemporary America." The arts properly belong among the basics—rather than being something apart from the Three Rs, the arts should be used as "powerful aids" for teaching them. He proposed a partnership of professional artists with teachers for the sake of children. "The tentative evidence is that [the arts] have had a remarkably constructive effect on both learning and behavior."

An article which preceded this one, called "Art for Math's Sake," was written by Luisa Kreisberg and appeared in *The New York Times* of April 25, 1976. "You can start with very young children to foster understanding of complex visual structures," writes Kreisberg. "Later that understanding can be applied in many ways. The artist's job, like the scientist's or mathematician's, is to make the invisible visible. Children can learn to better use their brains through their eyes."

When we saw our preschoolers' spellbound reaction over a period of an hour and a half to the visiting Bunraku Puppet Theater from Osaka, Japan, we understood what Barbara Tuchman meant in her important *New York Times Magazine* article of

November 2, 1980, "The Decline of Quality." She speaks of the urge for the best as "an element of humankind as inherent as the heartbeat. . . . How will the young become acquainted with quality if they are not exposed to it?" Certainly our preschool children *knew* that what they were experiencing with those remarkable puppeteers was something truly great, and they were entranced, even if they did not put that feeling into words.

Jacques d'Amboise is to dance what Suzuki is to the violin. With his National Dance Institute, he teaches thousands of children every year to love dancing. About a thousand of them are chosen at year's end to perform at Madison Square Garden's Felt Forum in what he calls, "The Event of the Year." (In 1986 he even invited and trained children from China, who had never been out of their country before—the show was called "China Dig"). Barbara Gelb writes of d'Amboise as the "Pied Piper of Dance" (*The New York Times Magazine,* April 12, 1981), saying that he dreams of "sweeping into rhythmic self-expression all the youth of America." Dancing, he feels, is every child's cultural birthright. "He has stayed close to the little boy within him, and that is the most compelling of his gifts as a teacher of children." Children view him as a "tall child" with whom they have a "delicious rapport." He owes his dance career to his mother, "who combined dreamy romanticism with concrete aspiration." He is trying to expose children to dance, not make dancers out of them, just as Suzuki exposes children to the violin without any expectations that they will become career violinists. "I try to make it an adventure for the children," says d'Amboise. Gelb describes a d'Amboise class with children as a combination of "cajolery, scolding, clowning, and praise," with no condescension. He is indeed the Suzuki of dance!

In *Let's Play Math,* Michael Holt and Zoltan Dienes point out: "Without the creative use of language, a child's gift of intelligence cannot mature." Games induce a child to "think with his hands." "Mathematics in particular requires strong links to be made between hands and brain for success." Parents should realize the tremendous value in playing with a child. Their interest is *very* important in the early stages of a child's life. "The adult has a much more vital role to play than 'nursemaid'—that of an encouraging, knowledgeable friend. . . . If a child can learn to speak by two all by himself, no wonder he can do so much more than we ever thought possible." It is striking to realize how many educators have used the same analogy to language learning that is so central to Suzuki's approach.

Under Five in Great Britain, by Jerome Bruner, is about his experiences living in England and observing English educational practices. He calls the "importance of early childhood for the intellectual, social and emotional growth of human beings . . . one of the most revolutionary discoveries of modern times. . . . The earlier a skill can be mastered without tears and sacrifice of other values, the more will it contribute to a child's life and form the basis of other skills. . . . One needs to ensure that parents keep confidence in their own skills as child rearers. . . . This may be the seed time for working out ways to give young children a better start and their families more heart in the future . . . the return in kindling human hope for the future would be great."

During the *MacNeill-Lehrer Report* on WNET-TV of September 13, 1977, Kenneth Kenniston, speaking of his study on families for the Carnegie Corporation, *All Our Children,* said it was impossible to expect two adults to bring up a child without help in America today. But he also affirmed that parents are "the world's greatest experts on the needs of their children. . . . The goal of public policy should be to build on and strengthen that expertise." This is the main goal of our Pre-School—to give parents, so justifiably overwhelmed, all the help we possibly can.

Remarks by Alan Pifer, President Emeritus of the Carnegie Corporation, from a speech to the Conference of Child Welfare League, "Children—A National Resource" (reprinted in *High/Scope Research,* October 1982), emphasize the broader humanitarian need to adopt ideas of the sort Suzuki advocates—and soon: "If we deny children's needs, we deny our humanity. The greatest need today is to re-establish respect for human worth. The vast majority of the world's people live under authoritarian regimes. A widespread decline in reverence for human life and loss of respect for the dignity of the individual has led to an indifference toward the welfare of children. Good preschool education and associated parent training is highly 'cost-effective.' Mothers must be the partners of teachers, and the key people in children's growth and development. In dedicating ourselves to children, perhaps we can start a general renaissance of the human spirit."

Finally let me close the chapter with a beautiful summary of Shin'ichi Suzuki's ideas by Suzuki himself: "The talent of a child is not inborn. Any child has the sprout of possibility to grow. If a child is left alone, his talent will wither. Nurture that sprout with overflowing love, and make the flower of hope bloom."

THE METHOD IN ACTION: VIOLIN TRAINING FOR STUDENTS AND PARENTS

This chapter may well be hard going for a reader not familiar with the Suzuki violin method or what is involved in the study of the violin itself. I include this step-by-step progression once in this book to give the clearest possible picture of the detail necessary for successful learning in one subject area. A similar one-step-at-a-time approach is translated to all subject areas in the Pre-School. Patience will reward the reader with understanding not only of step-wise progression in teaching and learning but also of the parent-student-teacher relationship so crucial to any Suzuki-based curriculum.

The violin, which can be made in tiny sizes without altering its playing characteristics, is an instrument that is well suited to young children. Its dependence on finger dexterity also reinforces the natural development of small-muscle coordination. The violin requires that correct pitch be produced by finding precisely the right point on a string for producing a given sound. It offers a child excellent training in aural sensitivity, since it requires him to compare constantly the sound he is producing with the correct pitch.

Violin is taught in several different forms in the Pre-School: semi-private lessons with a teacher, two parents, and two children; small group lessons with a teacher and several children; larger group lessons (about half the class) with a teacher, parents, and children; and the entire class working together with two teachers. In these ways, the children's violin experience is mostly with other children at about the same developmental level and is a part of each day in some way. Depending upon his birthday, a child may be part of our school for usually two and sometimes three years. Pre-Schoolers don't necessarily advance faster on the violin than music school students of about the same age, but they do seem to accept it more naturally as a normal part of their lives, something they never remember being without. One problem we continue to have is that when parents are attracted to the Pre-School for everything else it offers and consider the violin as merely an interesting bonus, they must be made aware of the enormous commitment required of them for their children to be successful on the instrument. If we are unsuccessful in convincing a parent of this, we are likely to see the child drop out, usually about a year after graduating from the Pre-School. The one thing that has been most reaffirmed over the years in our school is that if parents are deeply involved, their children succeed. When they are not, a child can struggle along for a while but sooner or later becomes too discouraged to continue. Luckily this kind of less-committed parent is very much in the minority at the school, and we teachers are hard on ourselves, too, when any child stops playing. I rejoice in the parents who delight in enjoying each learning step of their children, who may pass up apparently more "glamorous" career opportunities to concentrate on their children's learning, without, at the same time, allowing themselves to be swept up in a breathless competition for the title of Super Mom or Super Dad. The quietly devoted parents who have refused to be thrown into a tailspin by the crazy pace of the world around them are the ones who make our work so worthwhile, and it is their concern and attention— rather than their level of formal education—that we have found is most crucial.

New students are always put into a violin group by themselves to start. Depending upon their rate of progress, they are kept in this beginning group or transferred to the more advanced group. A few of our most advanced students are absorbed into afternoon music school group classes as well, making the transition to afternoon school particularly smooth.

Children's Classes

Violin group classes are a mixture of sitting, standing, and marching activities. We most often begin with some kind of general calisthenics to loosen up the muscles of the entire body and make minds alert. The whole class is conducted in a lively rhythm, with the teacher aware of each child's response. She must know how and when to change activities, and what preparations are necessary before each new learning step can be accomplished by the children. There are rhythmic games that loosen up the body and achieve good posture. Other games, often accompanied by songs, develop finger dexterity. It is the combination of relaxed bodies and quick response that makes for a good Suzuki violin class.

Quick response is the key to getting violins into Rest Position and then Playing Position on the count of "One, two, three!" I will often scramble the order of steps—"Stop!" (violin straight out in front of the child), "Turn!" (violin "head" aimed at floor), "Fly it into your nest!" (violin onto shoulder), and "Chin!" (head turned left, and jaw down onto chin rest)—to see if all the children are wide awake. Most often we teachers set bow grips over and over and then have parents do the same while we watch, to be sure this important position is clearly felt and understood. Bow exercises in the air often follow: Helicopters (up and down), Make a Breeze (out to the side and back in), and Stir the Pudding (circles in front of the body)—all done with the whole arm while the bow is held straight. Putting an imaginary orange on top of the bow gives children a sense of the balance essential to bowing. They love to "drop the orange" at the end of these exercises, with a quick flick of the wrist that is itself good practice for bowing. Paint Rollers (one hand on either end of the bow, while pretending to paint the room orange, or pink, or any other color) and Rocket to the Moon (bow straight up on top of the head, "like an antenna") are other good preparations for actual playing. But before we play, we often do Helicopters, landing straight down and silently with the bow on the A string—"without a sound," as we tell the children. From there we tip silently from string to string—E, A, D, G, D, A, E—and "don't make a sound!"

Finally we are ready for the playing of one repetition of the first *Twinkle* rhythm on the E string (first variation of the children's first piece, *Twinkle, Twinkle Little Star and Variations*). This is done in rhythm, following the teacher's example. For concentration and development of beautiful tone the best method is to do this all around the circle of children, without once letting the rhythm drop. It becomes a matter of honor among the students not to let the music stop. This up-to-tempo rhythm is in fact the most important element in all our violin and other teaching. Without that liveliness, learning grows very bogged down and burdensome. Children *know* when you are and are not with them, feeling their true rhythms and knowing their authentic concerns.

So that children do not become too tired in a standing position, some quiet but fast-moving finger games and songs often follow in a sitting position. We make "eyeglasses" with "thumb and one" (the index finger), "thumb and two" (the middle finger), and so forth, and then tap those fingers near our ears to hear the rhythm: "What are your fingers playing?" We also pat the rhythm on our knees, shoulders, head, or the floor before we clap it. The clapping motion is difficult at first for very young children. I often clap one repetition of a rhythm behind a child's back and wait for him to repeat it, always trying not to let the rhythm lag. At this point tuning forks may be introduced, the teacher first letting each child hear hers in his ear, then all the children "becoming" tuning forks with arms raised "vibrating" in the air, while singing "A string!" on the A pitch. We also sing the sounds of all the strings in another game: "E string, A string, D string, G string"—down and up and down again, while moving our bodies from up on tiptoes to curled up in a little ball on the floor and then extending back up to tiptoes again, in time with our rising and falling voices. We talk about the E string as being the roof of a building, the A string as the second floor, the D string as the first floor, and the G string as the basement. In these ways children become very familiar with the sounds of those open strings through both singing and pizzicato right from the very beginning. The sooner they know whether or not their violins are in tune, the better.

Children particularly love the tuning fork. They will work

hard to overcome the coordination obstacles to learning to use the fork, either to listen to the A pitch at their own ears or on the violin bridge, for enhanced tone. It is quite a trick for a two- or three-year-old child to give the fork a strong tap on the rug, holding it below the vibrating part so that when he turns the fork over and touches the violin bridge with the knob at the bottom of the fork the vibrations making the sound are not damped. When we let children struggle with this until they get it, their sense of accomplishment and delight in that beautiful reverberating sound shows that for them it was well worth all their trouble.

After a piano introduction and playing through the first variation of *Twinkle* on open E string, we offer the chance to play a solo, with or without the piano, to anyone who would like. We prefer to wind up the beginner's class with a march: this is a truly happy ending, and it leaves children wanting more. It frees both their bodies and their tone, as the calisthenics did at the beginning of the class. It is also wise to have lots of preparation for the final concert, when the whole school marches into the auditorium and up onto the stage playing the *Twinkle* variations. We get our "marching feet" ready by feeling the beat with feet "like drumsticks on a drum." I then do a lot of bowing the rhythm in the air and ask children to "follow the leader silently." I make sure I have "all eyes this way," so that in the event that hearing becomes difficult when we are all spread out over a long corridor or auditorium, children can catch the direction, speed, and rhythm of the leader's bow by watching. Aiming to be "like one violin—all together," we set off down the hall and back, sometimes up and down stairs as well. It takes a long time to coordinate this marching and playing at the same time, both physically and musically, but children love it and it brings happy tears to parents' eyes at concerts.

Observing good Suzuki-style teaching is better than reading about it! One must constantly go with the flow when very young children are concerned and be willing to give up each and every one of one's cherished lesson plans, changing gears in an instant if that is a better way to go with the children. Flexibility is everything in this (as I think it is in *all*) teaching.

Let me add here a note for those familiar with the Suzuki method for teaching the violin. The pre-violin box—perhaps a

Cracker Jack box with a small ruler attached as a "fingerboard," serves to introduce very young children to the experience of holding an instrument without imposing on them the weight of a real violin or the need to fit their jaws to the actual chin rest, which can take some getting used to. We have made a conscious decision not to use the pre-violin box in our classroom. This is mostly because of the bad experience of one child in a music school where I taught violin by the Suzuki method some years ago. Begun on a box violin and dowel-stick bow, this child "played" right through the advanced pieces in a group concert. But when she got her real violin and bow, she suddenly made the most horrible scratching sounds, being used to exerting pressure with her pretend bow and not listening for tone, since none was to be had. Her disillusionment took the better part of a year to overcome. Many fine Suzuki teachers *do* start children very successfully with the pre-violin, and we might well see a need to do so in the future. But for now, we would prefer to continue to be exceptionally careful how we prepare children and use the actual instruments. We want nothing to come between them and the real thing. At first only one small violin is passed around at the end of a beginning group class, in the very same way that Dr. Suzuki began his teaching after the war—because at that time he had only one violin available for his lessons. We are anxious to build eagerness in young children for their own instruments *before* they are given them, but we would rather not use any substitute for the instrument during that essentially pre-violin time.

The Progress of a Children's Class

To give an idea of the actual progress of a class, I offer below a record of a class of six children ranging in age from two-and-one-half years to three years of age which began in February 1976. The reader should understand that each time an activity is mentioned, that is the first time that activity has been introduced. He should also assume that each old activity is being repeated as the new ones are added. Often the children suggest or invent the activity, and the best Suzuki teachers follow the children's lead. Very likely the teacher will be able to work the class back to her ideas if she has imagination. Leading Suzuki classes with their fast

Dr. Suzuki with a Suzuki Pre-School student and mother at a Manhattan School ▶ of Music Workshop, April 1978.

Violin performance at The Suzuki Pre-School.

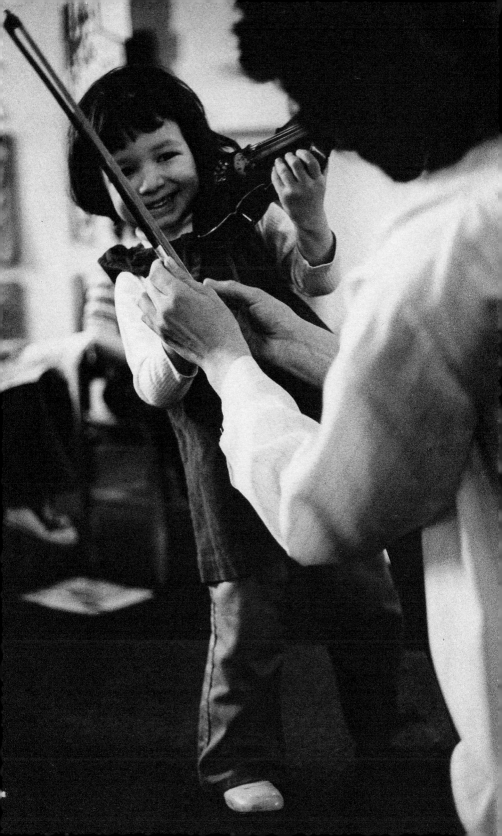

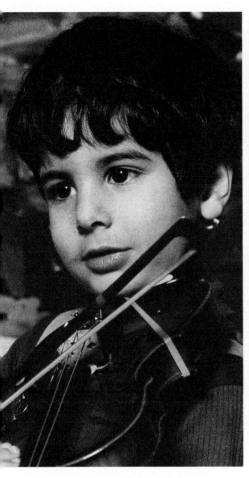

Violin classes at The Suzuki Pre-School.

Manhattan School of Music Workshop, April 1978. Teachers Margot Cohn and Susan Grilli with Suzuki Pre-School students.

◀ Violin group lesson.

Musical play and singing games in a violin group class with teachers Susan Grilli, Margot Cohn, and Marai Yaw.

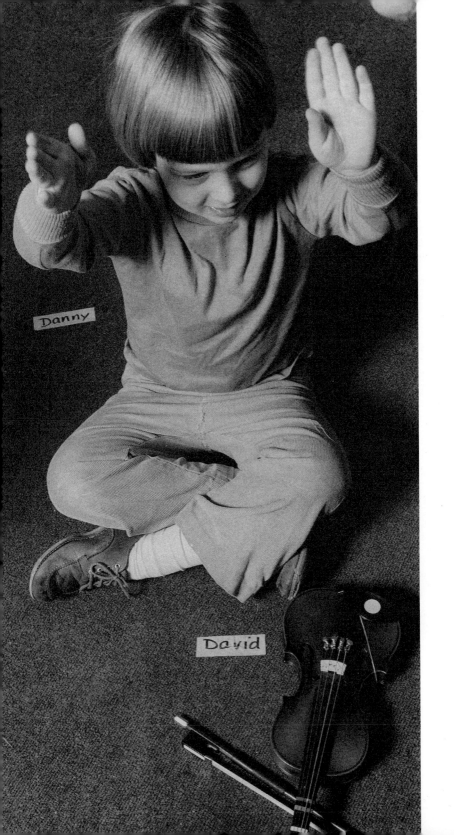

Danny

David

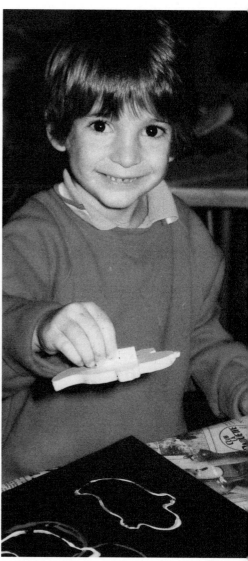

A natural and joyful concentration is the result when students are truly engaged
in a wide variety of challenging activities.

Above: Suzan Grilli with Dr. Suzuki in Matsumoto, Japan.

At left: Group demonstration at Manhattan School of Music Workshop, April 1978, with Susan Grilli and Dr. Suzuki.

Large muscle play, indoors and outdoors at The Suzuki Pre-School.

A student in a violin group class.

tempi and large amount of physical activity is an energetic business—some of the best teachers even teach in rhythm. They know a lagging pace can kill the process of learning. Children love having to react quickly and show they can be ready to play as fast as the teacher can count "One, two three!" The classes may be short, but they are lively and to the point. If they lack fun, something is wrong. Sharing this fun with parents can be the best part of all.

In the very first class, a parent was behind each child as the children sat in a circle. A violin case was in front of each child. The teacher said, "Take your baby (violin) out of the case and hold it in your arms." The children each had their own way of getting their violin out of their case: some instruments tumbled out onto the floor and others were so cautiously lifted out that it seemed to take forever. The teacher showed each child how to put his violin in rest position—"Make a cradle for the baby." The teacher then asked all the children to stand up with their violins and bow— "One (bending down), two (all the way down), three (back up again)." This was done several times, until all the children could do it. Then an open manila folder was put in front of each child, and the teachers helped them to set their feet on the folders, in playing position. The teachers drew around the feet with red magic marker. (The left foot is slightly ahead of the right, and the feet point out, with space between them.) The teacher told the children, "Get on your feet!" and began swaying back and forth rhythmically as she played *Twinkle, Twinkle Little Star* on her violin. Later, the parents stood in front of their children, holding their hands and swaying with them as the teacher played. The teacher told the children, "Float your violins gently down to the floor, like leaves in a breeze," and did so herself. The children followed, and put their "babies" to bed in the violin cases. Sitting in the circle, they sang *Twinkle* (in D-major, since A-major, the first key the children play in, is too high for singing). Then the teacher showed how she could cross her legs "Indian style" and with her hands tap a rhythm on her knees: "I like choc-'late ice cream," the rhythm of the first variation of *Twinkle, Twinkle Little Star,* which is the first piece in *Suzuki Violin School,* volume one. Only parents use the music. Children learn everything by ear until they have become quite advanced as players. The children listen to a recording of all the pieces in the first two books of *Suzuki Violin School,* and the more repetitions of this that take place at home the faster the child seems to learn. This first lesson ended with the same bow that began it, providing a neat beginning and ending for the class.

At the second lesson, we introduced the E string, and the teacher sang, "Where's your E string?" on the E pitch and in rhythm. She plucked her E string, and the children scrambled to find theirs, plucking a variety of strings in the process. But as she repeated and repeated the sound, now going around to each child in the circle and plucking E close to his ear, more and more children were able to imitate the sound with their own voices and find the E on their own instruments.

Next the tuning fork was introduced. The teacher tapped one of its prongs on the floor and turned it right side up on her violin bridge so the children could hear the A pitch of the violin's second string, the pitch always tuned first. Then she went around the whole circle doing this on each small violin and also letting the child hear the A in his ear. Many children wanted to try this themselves, so the tuning fork was later set out on the science table for exploration during Free Play.

Still sitting on the floor, the teacher stretched one hand as high in the air as she could and sang, "E string" ("Way up on the roof"),"A string" ("Second floor!"), "D string" ("First floor!"), and "G string" ("Way down in the basement!"). Then, without saying anything, she simply sang, "E string, A string, D string, G string, G string, D string, A string, E string!" and the children followed her with their hands and voices. This was repeated until everyone had it pretty well. This day the violin was put under the chin of each child as he stood on his "playing feet," just for a brief moment. The teacher then led a march after first establishing the basic beat by having the children march in place. The march went all around the room and ended up back on the playing feet. From there the teacher said, "Step off your playing feet, get kissing feet" (feet together), "and bow."

In the following days, more was said about opening violin cases only when the case was "on its feet," since opening it upside down invariably led to the violin tumbling out onto the floor. We also began the "Where is the . . . " game, from a sitting position, first with the violin and then with the bow. The teacher chanted rhythmically, "Where is the head?" and, with the children, "Here is the head!" (pointing to the violin scroll). The game continues with "Where is the bridge?" "Here is the bridge!" and so forth. Soon the children were all chanting along with the teacher in rhythm, straining to learn all the new words. What's especially fun about this game is that the last question, always asked in an exaggeratedly conspiratorial tone of voice, has a "don't" answer, which the children love. In reply to "Where is the hair?" they chant "*Don't* touch the hair! Don't touch the hair! Don't touch the hair!" while moving their hands *so* close to the bow's hair, but not quite touching it. A few children will always touch the hair, of course, but most play along for the sake of the surprise twist at the end, and they seem to love to keep up the rhythm of the game.

One day violin cases were placed behind each child, and we introduced a game for quick response that is the forerunner of Simon Says. Speed and close observation are essential for this game. The teacher directs it, saying, "Hands on your head!" "Hands way up tall!" "Hands on your shoulders!" and so on. Children respond well to this, building up speed as they repeat it.

Standing up very fast when the teacher said "One, two, three!" (she may give incorrect clues like "One, two eight!" or "One, two, five!" first), the children were now ready for "Get on your horse and grab your reins": The teacher played the fourth variation of *Twinkle, Twinkle Little Star,* the one with the sixteenth-note rhythm that we call "Lo-co-mo-tive," and bent her knees in time to it, feet planted in playing position. The children followed, grabbing the imaginary reins with their hands. This rhythm, like all others, is purposely taken at a good clip right from the beginning, so that when children finally put their bows on the strings of their violins, they can immediately play up to tempo. Suzuki's idea of preparing a note very carefully, then playing it right up to tempo, seems an excellent one to us. A small phrase, learned in this way, can be added to another small phrase, and so on, until a whole piece has been learned at its natural, lively speed.

An important step was taken next. Everyone stood up "One, two, three!" and the teacher said, "When you hear 'One, two, three,' get your violin in rest position!" Only one child could do this accurately at first. Others got the violin under the wrong arm, or turned around, or backwards. But with repetition and a lot of individual help all of them had the idea by the end of the class.

We began the next class by helping each child into rest position, saying, "Keep the baby in the cradle." Then, "Wave your free hand, your left hand!" At this point, both the teachers went around the circle making sure all the right hands were cradling the violins and all the left hands were waving in the air. Since the children seemed ready to go on, the teachers showed them how to bring their left hands down to their violin "shoulders," and "hold on tight." When everyone could do this, the teacher said, "Now wave your right hand!" Each child was shown how to do this, individually.

The next step, on another day, was to help the children put the left hand on the violin "shoulder," fix their feet in the playing position, wave their right hands, and bring their violins straight out (violin head up) over their left feet, saying, "Stop!—just the way the policeman stops traffic!" We could then go on still another day from "Stop!" practiced several times to "Stop!" "Turn!" (violin, head down), "Fly it in!" (into the "nest"—the perfect spot behind the collarbone where the violin sits comfortably). We repeated this over and over again, first with the whole group and then with individual children. Then the teacher added, "Cover your shoulder with your violin!" and "Chin!" —showing how by bringing her chin down into the chin rest.

We were ready now for "Stop! Turn! Fly it in! Chin! No hands!" (The clues that bring the child and his violin into the following position: The violin is in its perfect spot or "nest," the child turns his head left and puts his chin securely down on the chin rest. He then rests his left hand on his right shoulder, holding the violin with his chin alone—the way it will be held through all his playing to come.) We repeated this many times, each time giving the children a lot of individual help and carefully lining up the child's body so that head turned left would allow eyes to "look down the violin strings," the violin would be over the left foot, and posture would be straight and tall. To do this best, with an individual child, the teacher stands in front of him while he does "Stop! Turn! Fly it in!" and then moves to his left before he turns his head, so that he will preserve a good position and not have to lose it to watch the teacher. In a large group class, the teacher makes a point of directing the group from the children's left so that they can watch her, look down at their fingers, and look up to the teacher again.

At this same time we began certain games for finger dexterity, far before the time the children would need to know fingering on the violin. This needs much preparation, and we do it with clay and play dough and a finger strengthening toy just as much as with the games that are a part of the violin class. We began with *Eensy Weensy Spider* (sung with finger-play accompaniments, fingers moving individually and as fast as possible). Another song, which begins "One thumb, one finger, one hand, keep moving keep mov-ing," was even more popular at this stage. It is basically an arpeggio followed by a downward scale, and it closes with: "And we'll all be hap-py and gay!" This was difficult for the children for quite a while. We also played "I see you!" with this game, and then bounced the fingers in rhythm near our ears so that we could hear the "bounce, bounce" sound. Since the children become very quiet so they can hear the tapping sound of their fingers bouncing, this is an excellent game for listening and observation.

Before introducing the bow, we added the rest of the *Twinkle* rhythms to our clapping. The children especially enjoyed singing the second variation to their own names: "My name is Douglas, and my name is Mara, and . . . " while the teacher points to each child in the circle as the song continues, all the while trying to keep the rhythm from faltering. For the rhythm of the third variation we used, "Run, Jim-my" and for the fourth, "Lo-co-mo-tive" or "Wa-ter-mel-on" (since many of the children didn't know what a locomotive was!) We then began passing the rhythm around the circle and found it was extremely difficult for the children to clap just one rhythm as the teacher pointed to them around the circle. It was some time before they could do this, and when they finally mastered it and didn't lose the beat, they were delighted. This achievement came first with "the name game" (the second rhythm, described above), probably because it was personal and important to them.

The teacher introduced the bow, first through small-sized Dixie cups—each child had one put in his hand as he stood in a circle. She went around pretending to pour each child's favorite juice into each cup. Then she raised the cup straight into the air and back down again very slowly, "like an elevator." "Now, stir a giant pudding," she said, keeping her cup in an upright position—

"Don't spill the juice!"—and making large, very relaxed circular motions out to her side, around to the front, and back in toward her body again, over and over. "Now, make a breeze!" (out and in motion, to the side, arm very relaxed and free). "You can spill just a little juice now." The teacher showed what she meant by rotating her hand just enough to tip the cup over and quickly back up again. Of course the children were delighted with this and spilled a lot more juice than the teacher! The teacher "refilled" all the juice cups, and the exercises for developing precise yet free movement of the bow arm and hand were repeated, the children taking tremendous strides in just this one short lesson.

Another day we began with "pretend cups" for these exercises and soon graduated to real bows, not wanting to stay with substitutes for long because we find the children do better if they become acquainted with the real equipment as soon as possible. The teacher went around the circle setting each bow grip individually, as perfectly as possible, and told each child to freeze the good position, "like a statue." With his bow resting on his left shoulder, a child can see what he is doing when he fixes his bow grip, so we have used this most often. From there, the first rhythm is played right on the shoulder, and it is an easy step for the teacher to position the child's violin right under the bow and help him play his first "I like choc-'late ice cream" on the open E string. That is a moment for a camera, though we never seem to have one handy: the children's eyes light up so at those first sounds! And what broad, *unbelieving* grins!

The rhythms can all be played on the child's rosin as he is rosining his bow each time he gets it out to play. "Ros-in in your left hand, bow is in your right hand" is a refrain children enjoy singing to the tune of the first variation. On the violin, the teacher helps the child play "Only on the E string," and puts a tape "highway" on his violin between the bridge and the fingerboard to show where the bow should "travel."

The teacher then taught the children to get into rest position with both violin and bow, bow on the "bow hook"—index finger sticking out from the hand "cradle." From here on in, classes always began with this complete rest position, unless there was still a special need to work on either bow or violin alone. In order not to take the children ahead too fast with violin and bow, we often backtracked with more complicated variations on games we had played before. This is the point where it is all too easy to rush ahead too fast, spoiling all the careful preparation that has gone before. Another such point comes when the children first learn to use left-hand fingers. If that is rushed, the consequences can be terrible for all of the child's future playing, for the bad sound of sloppily prepared playing may discourage him from picking up his violin at all.

A popular game with the children was "What string am I playing?" The teacher went behind each child's back so he couldn't see which string it was. Most could guess at least the two top strings. The less familiar D and G strings will be introduced much more intensively when the time comes to teach the child his first pieces in D-major and G-major—not for a long, long time. Variations on this game were plucking an open string behind a child's back and clapping a rhythm in the same way—"Can you copy my rhythm?" The children also sang along with all the rhythms as the teacher played them on her violin.

As preparation for later fingering, it is possible to start having the children sing the finger numbers they will be fitting to their first variation—"A-E-1-E-3-2-1-A," for example. The teacher can also play "Twinkle Sandwich." The first phrase, "top piece of bread" is, "A-E-1-E-3-2-1-A." The second phrase, or "first piece of baloney," is "E-3-2-1" and is repeated, and the last phrase, "bottom piece of bread," is just like the first one.

A game to see if the teacher can "get a free violin" is fun to play when the parents are in the class. They gently try to pull away the child's violin, to see if his chin is really holding it. This testing of how the child holds his violin is essential, since the hands must be free for fingering and bowing, and the arms and shoulders must be relaxed. The chin must have a good grip from the beginning; the No Hands game, or holding the violin with the chin alone, makes practicing this particularly enjoyable. As soon as she sees that the children are confident enough about holding the no-hands position, the teacher pulls away any violin that is too loosely held or "drooping like a necktie." The first time she tries this, she's likely to end up with an armful of tiny violins and a roomful of giggling children. She may let a child take her violin away to show what happens when your chin stops working. Children love it when the teacher needs help. They love to help her fix her bad position, and they usually improve their own positions in the process.

The teacher then began playing rhythms in the air with her bow—"Can you guess what I am playing?" Then the child who guessed the correct rhythm had a chance to play his violin alone with the piano, the teacher helping him to keep his bow on the E string. This solo playing went on for a long time because the children were not yet ready to play in unison. By guiding the child's bow arm, the teacher can give him the idea of pulling sound out of the string instead of pushing and scratching.

The teacher introduced pizzicato. The child sings "E string, A string, D string, G string," as he plucks twice for each string. The child turns his right thumb upside down and rests it on the violin fingerboard. With his index finger he gently moves along the string, under it, and lifts it up—letting it go, "ringing like a bell." Most children try this pretty roughly at first, then experiment to find how to make a better sound. The teacher is constantly setting an example of that sound on her own violin ("Can you match my tone?"), and teaches the parents to do the same when they work with their children at home.

Bow exercises done at first with cups, then pretend cups, are now done with the real bow. Some new exercises were added: Windshield Wipers, Paint Rollers, and Helicopters. Windshield Wipers involves rotating the arm and thus the bow, out and back in, to touch the strings. To do Helicopters, the child holds the bow horizontally, above the strings, and moves it straight up and down, up and down until at a signal from the teacher, who is doing the same thing, he brings it down, "straight down, like a helicopter coming in for a landing, not like an airplane," silently onto the string, "without a sound." The child holds both ends of the bow for Paint Rollers, moving it up, out, and back to him in large, relaxing circular motions. All of these exercises are designed to free the bow arm, yet make bowing precise.

After the children could land the bow silently on the A string (the most direct line for the "helicopter" to take from above the violin, since the arm would have to tip down for the E string), the teacher led them in tipping silently from string to string, "no squeaking." Most children make "scrunch" noises in their string crossing at first, but it soon becomes a matter of pride to do this quickly, noiselessly, and longer than anyone else. The children liked seesawing with the bow "without a sound" all the way over to the G string and back up to E. Getting faster and faster at it, they show they already have a good amount of control over the bow. (They couldn't do this if they had a "grabby" bow grip, for they would not have the proper balance.)

The day before we had the class play together with the teacher, she let each child try following her individually, as in a Suzuki private lesson. Teacher and child went through the steps for getting the violin into playing position together, then she said, "Rest your bow on E. Listen." (She played one clear repetition of "I like choc-'late ice cream"). "Ready-and-play" (said in rhythm), and the child played the rhythm "just once." The children lifted their bows "like helicopters" off the string together, got into rest position, and bowed. It was necessary for each child to practice this extensively. When he could follow the teacher's lead in this way, he had clearly accomplished a tremendous lot of learning for his age.

Growing quite a bit more expert, the children were now able to sit and clap rhythms (with hands together, not hands on knees), changing rhythms with the teacher without losing the beat. Some fell behind, of course, but they would catch up again and seemed to enjoy this game very much. Sustained playing in a group has only recently been attempted. Although the school year has a few weeks yet to go, the children can be expected to reach the point where they can play all the rhythms on the E string by June. The children who began in the fall of the previous year are at various stages of learning all the variations of *Twinkle*, with fingering. This progress may seem very slow, but it is wonderful to see the children building a really solid foundation, so that new pieces may be learned much faster!

Violin Classes for Parents

Suzuki often says to young students, "I am the teacher only one day a week. Your mother is the teacher six days a week!" In their own violin class, parents learn the basics of violin technique—enough to play through the children's first piece, the *Twinkle* variations. We make it clear from the start that we are not training parents to become accomplished violinists but rather so that they can teach their children at home. Parents share their new learning experience with their children, and children help parents to learn. One two-and-one-half-year-old girl was overheard saying to her mother, "Mommy, I like to play baby violins with you!"

We have found it is important to teach the parents very carefully, so that they thoroughly understand how to approach the teaching of their children at home. They need to be taught in basically the same way as the children, with faster progress inevitable and an open forum available for asking the "whys" of what we do, and how we do it. (Japanese parents are generally quite happy never to ask why and are phenomenally good at imitating precisely the teacher's playing, but American parents must know the reason behind everything, and we as teachers should be sure to give it to them.)

The first lesson began rather uncertainly when the teacher made the mistake of starting right out trying to teach the difficult art of tuning. The parents' instruments were cheap "boxes" made in Shanghai, with the cheapest possible strings on them. Before the teacher could caution about turning the pegs very slowly, going only a tiny distance before pushing the peg in to secure it, several parents had enthusiastically turned their pegs rather fast and far. The teacher had no chance to recover from the surprise of seeing three strings break in one minute before another two went— and with them her dignity and professional poise. Trying to reassure the parents that this was certainly unusual, she took up one of their violins and confidently began to tune it, when "Pop!"— another string gone! Reduced to giggles and unable to keep up with repairing the destruction, we gave up for that day, and it seemed that the parents' confidence in playing this new and strange instrument was shaken, even if their sense of humor was not. Rule number one: Find good instruments with good strings or a sympathetic rental company, like ours, that will replace every misbehaving part free of charge.

The real beginning of the parents' violin classes came the following week. The teacher tuned all the instruments (now with new strings) and began by having the parents get into rest position with their violins alone. The parents went through the motion of bowing with feet together that they had seen their children do, and the teacher explained why we were using the bow: not to copy Oriental habits but rather to give a neat beginning and ending to each class. The teacher set each violin "in the nest" and watched each parent try this, to see if they understood how to find that special spot. It took several lessons to establish this firmly. The parents generally were anxious, in a way their children never were, about learning the violin. Of course this is natural, and the teacher's job is as much to relax them and make them enjoy this experience they will be sharing with their children as it is to teach the techniques of violin playing. At each lesson, we began with limbering up exercises—stretching up as tall as possible, then scrunching down, then back up again. Since the parents were very afraid of dropping their violins, we did many repetitions of "Stop! Turn! Fly it in! Chin!" right from the beginning, so they could feel their jaws holding the violins securely. It seemed the faster parents performed these steps the more accurately they got their violins over their shoulders. A fast-paced class that left them no time for worrying about what they were doing was even more important for them, it seemed, than for their children. The teacher kidded them about clenching their teeth to "help" hold the violin by doing it herself and showing them how it looked. With this, the class really relaxed for the first time, and we began to have fun.

Soon parents could do exercises with "pretend cups" to get the soft and round feeling needed for a comfortable bow grip, one where the balance of the hand on the bow provides control. The teacher set each bow grip as she did for the children, with bows resting on left shoulders. Only one parent had a very tense, grabbing kind of bow hold. The teacher worked more with her than with all the others on this, wanting her to be able to show her child the correct, more relaxed hold—and to feel it herself as well. As soon as she was shown that it was the positioning of the fingers on the bow that determined the control, she began to lose that tension, and now she is playing very freely, all the way through the *Twinkle* variations.

By the third lesson, the "no hands" position was comfortable for most parents, bows were set on the E string, and the teacher helped each parent feel the bow hairs sinking into the string as they pulled out the sound of the open string, using the first rhythm. The parents were as pleased as the children with these first sounds. The teacher stressed the idea of pulling rather than pushing, holding back each parent's bow as they pulled it to give them a feeling of resistance. During the same lesson the "open up your elbow" and "bounce a pretend ball" ideas helped give parents the relaxed feel of a bow arm in motion: The teacher tells them, "Open up your elbow," and they are shown how to extend the bow arm straight out from the shoulder and then "bounce a ball"—as if dribbling a basketball straight up and down in front of the body with the bow arm. The mid-point of each parent's bow was taped to show where to start playing. I explained that everyone had a different "middle of the bow," since this was measured by the square of their particular arm with the violin as they held the bow on the string. The next step was for the teacher to let each parent try playing several repetitions of the first rhythm on the E string, alone—for tone and for precision of rhythm. Then, while the teacher played the first phrase of the first variation of *Twinkle*, the parents played it on the open E string. The aim was always a big, clear tone. Although the children had freer bow arms right from the beginning (something the parents had to develop), a lot more work on developing beautiful tone can and should be done with parents, since they will be teaching their children at home and setting an example for them. The teacher, for instance, frequently went around the circle of parents, stopping and playing a rhythm to be immediately copied by that parent. She then tried playing with the parents one at a time in the circle without dropping the rhythm. They were delighted to be able to do this, if exhausted from the effort. It was then possible to have parents play one at a time around the circle, without the teacher's example, taking care not to let the rhythm falter.

By this time, the parents could play all the rhythms on both the E and A strings. As they became more proficient at this, the teacher began to play a piano accompaniment to their open-string rhythms, and even to switch rhythms on the piano and have the parents follow without losing the beat.

When parents were able to tip the bow from one string to another without extraneous sound, they had accomplished clean string crossings. When a good clear tone had been achieved, the teacher put left-hand finger tapes on the violin fingerboard. In preparation for using fingers to press down strings, the teacher showed the parents how to practice a "throw down, spring back" motion of their fingers on the violin shoulder before moving the hand down fast (so as not to lose the position of fingers "on heads," which is needed for proper fingering) to where the tapes are. The first finger was then bounced "on its head" on the first E-string tape, then the second was added, then the third. The parents practiced putting first, second, and third fingers down, in that order, as quickly as possible. They built up good speed in this over a few weeks, and only one still put all her fingers down in a block because we were going too fast for her to perform the correct "one, two, three" sequence. The same exercises were done on the A string. The ideas "finger first, then bow" and "bow, fingers—same string," were as helpful to the parents as they are to children. The teacher even used the same train analogy with the parents as with the children: "Stop the train (the bow) to let the people (fingers) get on or off!"

The teacher then led the parents in a scale using fingers, up and down the A and E strings. She had them stop between each note to prepare for the next one (finger first, then bow). Then, again with stops, they played the first variation of *Twinkle,* the teacher saying the finger number of each note before it was played and keeping the rhythm going. Several teaching aids help at this point. One is a drawing of the musical staff showing the A-major scale, and indicating which notes are on A and which on E strings. Another is a drawing of the four violin strings and position of fingers on them, with numbers and note names provided. For easier learning of *Twinkle,* a picture of "the Twinkle Sandwich" shows very graphically a slice of bread, two slices of baloney, and another slice of bread. Each sandwich layer has a phrase of *Twinkle* written on it (the notes in that phrase, by number.) By the last week in April, the parents were itchy to stop the "stops" between notes in *Twinkle* and play the piece all the way through. By mid-May they could play all the variations with piano accompaniment.

On our last day of school, the children and parents give a concert together, the parents playing *Twinkle* with fingers and the children on open strings (except for the older ones who have learned fingers already and may play special solos). With the addition of an art exhibit of children's paintings, and pretzels and butter the children make themselves, this event is a lot of fun.

The parents say they very much enjoy this experience of sharing learning with their children, and that is as it should be.

A SUZUKI-BASED PRESCHOOL CURRICULUM

Our curriculum is based on acceptance of the child and his schedule for learning. We affirm where he is now in his development and help him to take one new step in learning. We respect him for the enormous energy and determination he puts into finding out about the world around him, and we try to encourage him in Suzuki's "habit of action": the willingness to explore something new in as rich an environment as possible. There is plenty of time for exposure to this environment. When the child has absorbed all he can, he is ready for actual instruction, and we must be on the spot to teach him when he needs it and then only as much as he really needs. We are concerned with a child's whole educational environment. In working with parents to assure them of the crucial importance of what we are doing together for their children, we are aiming at Suzuki's "total education," education of the whole person.

In applying many of Dr. Suzuki's concepts of education in a general preschool setting, we have found that the same desirable abilities we aim to develop in children through the Suzuki method of music teaching—memory, coordination, quick response, careful observation, pride in accomplishment—can also be developed through math, science, art, and language. Although music remains at the heart of The Suzuki Pre-School program, it is just one part of a comprehensive preschool curriculum.

There is absolutely nothing stopping us from taking more care and courage in every choice we make for our children. We simply must choose fewer and better activities for children, and leisurely explore with them those few chosen programs in far greater depth. There is also nothing stopping us from setting an example for children of determination to do something— anything—*well,* with energy and good humor, especially if it does not at first succeed. There is something wonderful about learning to concentrate, listen, or memorize with such centeredness that you are not distracted by anything else going on around you.

What is stopping us from making all education as lively and fun as it is full of content? A friend, a Kabuki actor, commented when asked how he'd developed his enormous discipline at a young age: "They (the older actors who were his teachers) always made it fun for me, so I'd want to do more. I got hooked, and then there was no stopping me!"

The ideal learning atmosphere must be one which is in itself a microcosm of the best of the world outside, where each child contributes uniquely to the richness of a school society almost as important to him as his own home family. When I see a new child coming to school, I think with awe of all that we will share together, and how deeply I will come to know him.

General Principles and Aims

Picking the perfect mix of stimulation and relaxation for the Pre-School diet is a subtle challenge. Young children are refreshingly straightforward. (In settling disputes, they have a basic fairness to their approach that adults would do well to copy.) They also know when they are being bored, and they will walk right out on you if you are not interesting or if you are pushing them too much. The ultimate indicator of what curriculum directions to take is direct observation of the children. If you are a Suzuki-method teacher, you already know how flexible you must be, ready at any moment to throw out all your favorite lesson plans and follow children where they're really ready to go. This need for flexibility is multiplied many times over in a preschool setting, where you are dealing with all areas of learning. You neither want to patronize nor overexpose children.

The atmosphere of the class is important: it must be hard-working yet relaxed and with much room for humor. As teachers, we seem to get farthest when we adopt a fairly matter-of-fact tone with children. If we gush enthusiasm or overpraise when children know perfectly well it wasn't *that* good, they tend to take us less seriously. We also have to remind ourselves constantly not to talk too much. Doing and showing are far better than over-explaining.

Our practice of putting the students into "family groupings" of two-year olds with three-, four-, and even five-year olds works well for us. Older children gain enormously in confidence by learning to become good teachers of younger children, and younger children draw inspiration from more advanced work. A school in which children two and one-half to twelve years old work together with adults of all ages could be a very exciting place indeed!

We ask children to reach and search intellectually without losing sensitivity to the relationship of their lives to others and to the world around them. It would be impossible to give proper credit to all the many people who have given us ideas for our curriculum, either directly or indirectly. When you begin to see what children are really capable of, you realize there is no limit to this search. That is the excitement of involvement in a school like ours: as a teacher you must grow with the children. From our Suzuki violin teaching we have learned the rhythmic pace that is the key to keeping instruction lively. In fact, learning often seems to happen better at a quicker pace when minds are working fast and there is no time for doubts and fears to creep in. As a teacher, you find yourself guided by the natural learning tempo of the children themselves.

Effective step-by-step learning can only happen when basic teaching ideas are isolated and fed to children, using analogies from their own experience. By identifying the important preparation a child needs to take a new step in learning, we can make his job a lot easier. Skipping steps and necessary preparation gets children into trouble in their effort to understand. It is up to us to be sure we don't settle for these shortcuts; they are the beginning of the need for remedial work. It is when learning is made unnecessarily difficult for a child that he begins to hate it. The burden of making him successful is squarely on us.

There appears to be nothing a child cannot learn if it is presented in an appropriate way. To experience this, you must do your own analysis to find which preparations are necessary for each child. And this is possible only through careful observation and recording of children themselves. Keeping a notebook with a page for each child is a good idea, as difficult as it is for a teacher to stop and jot down even quick thoughts. You'll find you have a better picture of the child over time, if you do this. The case study in chapter 5 is an example of the insights this method can provide.

Scheduling

A typical three-hour morning in the Pre-School begins before all the children arrive, with two parents and two children sharing a private violin lesson of half an hour with each teacher. The rest of the children arrive and sign in. They then find an area of interest to them in either of the rooms set up for Free Play. This is perhaps the most important part of the morning, in which activities in many diverse subject areas are carefully geared to the changing needs and interests of the children. Here, the teacher must be most sensitive to where the child really is in his development, not only where he *seems* to be. If projects have been set up thoughtfully, some of the most interesting art, language, science, math, or music can come out of this highly concentrated free-choice period of the day. During this time one teacher takes a different small group each day for a violin class.

After Free Play, we all come together in what has become known as Circle Time. Here we share personal experiences, stories, poems, singing, violin games, theater games, the work that came out of Free Play, and occasionally the presentation of a special visitor. At this time we'll present the special project planned for after a cookie-and-juice break. After their snack the children go into the reading corner where they choose their favorite books and "read" to themselves while listening to recorded music. The in-depth project, usually in art, that follows gives the children a chance to work together uninterrupted for at least half an hour. We have often divided this project so that older children do it separately from younger ones, giving us a better chance to work in a more concentrated fashion with individual children at their own levels. We tell stories and play educational games of all sorts with the group not doing the project, then switch the two groups. When some of the children near kindergarten age, we take them separately for pre-reading and math work.

If the weather is good, we go outside to play on climbing equipment for the last half-hour. In bad weather we play circle games, mat games, on indoor climbing apparatus, or dance to recorded (usually ballet) music. When we're inside, we try to end with a quiet story so the children will be calm when their parents come to meet them.

Once a week parents spend the first hour in school sharing a violin class with their children, then taking their own violin instruction. Once a month, they join in a parents' discussion group led by a teacher on a specific topic. We give parents their own violin class only in their first year with us. After that we help them as needed as a part of their children's private lessons. Eurhythmics (an organic method for learning the meaning of musical notation through body movement) for children and a voluntary parents' class are offered on Fridays, though we would like to have it daily. Fridays are also Show-and-Tell days, when children bring something they have made at home or found in nature to share with the class. (We banned toys from Show and Tell when competition for the best and the latest grew too fierce and unfriendly.)

Scheduling at The Suzuki Pre-School has naturally been through enormous changes, depending upon our location and the number of children and teachers we have worked with. We've gone from fitting parents into the school schedule a full day a week to making them teaching assistants on a rotating basis to having them spend an hour a week in school (mandatory) and visit one whole day a month (or as their time permits). Parents sign up to spend a whole day in school whenever they can, but they are extremely busy, and for some this is nearly impossible. It is such a wonderful experience for both parent and child, however, that we keep encouraging it. Parents have regularly scheduled private violin lessons with their children, and more scheduling is necessary when older preschoolers join more advanced music-school violin groups in addition to their Pre-School violin class. The mandatory hour a week that parents spend in school is devoted to violin work, with and without their children, and parent discussions. When we can again find a Eurhythmics teacher to teach full-time, a wonderful precedent set by our first Eurhythmics teacher, we would like to do Eurhythmics with parents and children, Suzuki style. (For a further discussion of Eurhythmics, see pp. 91–92).

We offer parents occasional workshops in special subject areas such as mathematics, and these are most conveniently scheduled for our June Workshop week. Once a year we try to turn over the Pre-School classroom to parents to explore the materials and equipment however they like in a sort of adult Free Play session. This is glorious fun for all of us, but provokes a real crisis in scheduling, since the children have to move out to make way for their parents! Parents need more and more of these experiences and opportunities to try their hands at teaching in all subject areas, using the Suzuki approach. Doing it for oneself is far better than reading or hearing about it.

At The Day School, where three violin teachers shared the work of a twenty-four-child nursery, scheduling was at its most complex. We experimented with programs based on two and four days of violin practice. We divided the group into thirds, so each teacher in effect had her own small class. The space was long and narrow and allowed for little full-group activity. With so many children in that space, it was necessary to be very precise about exactly when and where each teacher would be doing what, and with which children. For twenty-four children it soon became clear it was realistic to fit in only two violin classes a week, since the school also offered gymnastics and Eurhythmics, which we did not want the children to miss. (We also had to fit in a weekly violin class for parents.) Our present schedule reflects our more relaxed environment and the availability of a greater number of spaces for learning, another important consideration in developing a working curriculum.

The Physical Setting: Space and Equipment

As The Suzuki Pre-School has moved from one location to another over the years, we have had to adapt to a number of different physical settings and arrangements. Now we have the use of five classrooms, one of which holds the bulk of the Pre-School equipment. Since the whole space is multi-use, a certain amount of packing away is necessary each night, and more on weekends. But this is nothing compared to our experience at the Cathedral, where we had to pack away every piece of equipment right down to tables, chairs, and even rugs—every day! The same was true to a lesser degree at School for Strings, where we used a waiting room and large group class/concert room—both of which had to be completely cleared of our (then less extensive) equipment each day. At School for Strings we reversed the procedure somewhat, clearing the waiting room of chairs before Pre-School equipment could be put out.

At The Day School we began with afternoon use of space another group used in the morning. Then we were hired by the school to run its own Nursery, so the space didn't have to be cleared at all—a great relief. (Those were the "good old days," when we even had janitorial help after each session.) At The Day School, as well as two long and narrow rooms with bathroom and sink right there where we needed them, we had the use of two outdoor play areas, city style (at the back and on the roof of the brownstone occupied by the school).

At the Cathedral of St. John the Divine, large storage cabinets were constructed on opposite walls of our rented basement hall at Synod House. This immense and imposing room had been built to seat six hundred at dinner, and it had become a multi-use space in a big way—we were as likely as not to have to clean up after another group before setting up for the day, and dragging all that furniture in and out of those cabinets each day was exhausting. (Yet we were rather proud of having gotten the process down to a fast-paced ten minutes!) We made a room within a room, with specially chosen modular and portable equipment (built to last, by Community Playthings), so that the school space would be a smaller, warmer, and more welcoming one for children. We had a lot of trouble satisfying city permit requirements for adequate lighting in this half-underground space, and we had to greatly increase the candlepower of already existing church fixtures and add our own lights. Use of the Cathedral School playground was a delight, with its imaginative and sturdy wooden climbing apparatus for use by children of all ages, and swings—by far the best playground equipment we've ever enjoyed. The perfect school, we've come to conclude, would have elements from all our four locations.

At the Aldersgate Church, the Pre-School has the use of five light and airy rooms. Outside of locking up violins and a tape recorder, a minimum of equipment is put away each day—a bit more on weekends, when the church uses the space for Sunday School. A wall cabinet (much like those at the Cathedral) was built in one room so that equipment we can't fit in the main Pre-School room can be stored out of sight while the church makes use of the space. Outdoors is a huge, unfenced and grassy area onto which we've put three pieces of tough tubular aluminum climbing equipment—a jungle gym and slide with walkway (Community Playthings), and Geodome (Constructive Playthings). All are portable.

Our rooms now are set up purposely to encourage moving equipment from one center of interest to another as learning moves in that direction. A block construction that is especially ambitious can be remembered better if paper and magic markers can be brought over to make a drawing of it. A hand print done with paints at the easel can lead to printing with sponge shapes from the math table, and dramatic play, whenever and wherever it happens, has to draw on equipment from all parts of the school. The bulk of our teaching equipment is in the Pre-School room. In this room are all table games, books, art supplies, musical supplies, dramatic play furniture, teachers' materials and small library of teaching ideas, and most of our furniture: a piano, three tables, chairs, a doll house, a puppet theater, a water table, art carts, a bookcase, a "kitchen," easels, bulletin and blackboard room dividers, and most cabinets. A room next door is where we keep sets of regular and large (hollow) blocks, legos, and dramatic play dress-up clothes. This is also where we do most art projects and have our snacks. Across the hall is the room used for climbing, riding, and balancing equipment. It contains gym mats and is also used for Eurhythmics, painting murals, dancing, and water play at a water table. The room is used, too, for private and group violin lessons. Down the hall is the Choir Room, used for children's and parents' violin lessons and parents' discussion sessions. This room is also sometimes used for special visitors' presentations, when they do not fit easily into the Pre-School room. (The Pre-School room will occasionally be the site of violin and Eurhythmics classes, but scheduling children into other rooms can be a problem when one group wants to use this most richly equipped room of all for a special activity that doesn't require all that equipment.)

We have the use of the church kitchen for storing the week's juice supply and for special cooking or science projects with the children. A large downstairs hall can be rented by the school for workshops, concerts, and such events as an international dinner, occasions when the entire school (Pre-School and music school parents, teachers, and students), is invited.

Perhaps it is my years spent in Japan that make me want to give our American children quality materials and more finely developed small muscle coordination. There is something magic about the capability of Japanese hands, and you rarely see self-conscious clumsiness there; instead there is a sort of national pride in what hands can do. Although I don't want to make copies of Japanese children or classrooms here in America, I can't help wanting some of that Japanese coordination skill and quickness for our children. Because the violin requires such an extraordinary degree of coordination, we have from the first been looking for manipulative toys and tools that would aid children in building finger dexterity and strength. The first such toy we bought for the school was a plastic ball with "feet" on springs, sticking out from all sides of it. The resistance you feel when you push these "feet" all the way down to the ball, is similar to the feeling you need in your left-hand fingers for the "throw down, spring back" motion in violin playing.

Using really sharp Fiskars scissors while warning the children to be careful with them has meant that they have a good tool to work with right from the beginning and really learn how to use scissors. Sharp scissors work properly, and in far more sophisticated ways than the "clunkers" that pass for scissors in many early childhood classrooms. Providing small artists' paintbrushes and watercolor sets of the best quality we can afford as well as the larger brushes and tempera paints used with easels or in mural painting gives children real media to learn to control. With our sculptor's clay, we use real sculptor's tools. In fact shopping at a local discount art supply store gives us lots of ideas for experimenting with new tools and materials in the classroom—equipment that would never appear in school catalogues or school supply stores. We use the thin magic markers as well as the thick ones and pencils fat and thin.

Buying good art supplies is an expensive but worthwhile endeavor—art work is more fun, more concentrated, and the product is far more beautiful. Contrary to a popular notion that children are only interested in the *process* of working in art, we find they are just as delighted with the *product*. We use magic markers, pastels, Craypas, and pencils for drawing, trying to find good colors in these, as well as in paints and construction paper. We never use newsprint, having sacrificed too many drawings to discoloration and tearing. We go to wholesale paper suppliers for everyday drawing paper and art stores for better drawing and painting pads.

Other materials and learning supplies are described below, together with the activities in which they are used.

The Range of Activities

It is difficult if not impossible to categorize strictly according to subject area the activities that fill the Pre-School day and year, since ideally each activity combines many different subjects and skills. But in spite of their natural overlapping, I would like to try to give an idea, at least, of the range of our activities across subject areas below. In the section that follows this, I will describe activities with the emphasis on their natural integration.

We do endless reading to the children to develop their language abilities. Children play with words tirelessly, twisting them and turning them to suit their whimsy. They love the game we play where we start a story and they have to finish it using their imagination. Children "read" to other children stories they have memorized and dictate to the teachers stories they have made up. Stories with a refrain, like "Hundreds of cats, thousands of cats, millions and billions and trillions of cats," from Wanda G'ag's *Millions of Cats,* or the refrain from the well-known story of the Gingerbread Man, "Run, run as fast as you can, you can't catch me, I'm the Gingerbread Man!" are particularly popular. A favorite with the children is Maurice Sendak's *Chicken Soup with Rice,* all of which they try to chant.

We encourage exploration of letters, making lotto-style matching games for letter recognition and preparing teacher created "books" on individual letters as needed. We label objects in the classroom and help children with their own beginnings at writing. We make a continual effort to place a pencil (or a paintbrush) correctly in a child's hand. He might as well learn this right from the very beginning. Teachers print words children request on special cards, and children participate in creating their own dictionaries.

Telling a story while illustrating it on a roll of shelf paper is one way to engage children's rapt attention, and you don't have to be a professional artist to enjoy doing this in a perfectly adequate, simple way (children like to see you learning too). In general, telling a story while looking at the children has a more direct impact on them than reading it. Children love to hear teachers and parents tell stories from their own lives: We had an owl at our house that we heard every night at the same time, and then one night a bright light was turned on in the neighborhood that hit the tree where the owl liked to perch, and we never heard him again. I related this story to the children, and they were drawn into it. Each day they wanted to know if the owl had come back. Many a picture comes from these stories.

Parents have occasionally made charming books of their own that tell of their children's experiences—efforts that pleased the children so much that they wanted to learn to read them. This is also the result of children making their own books. If they want to learn a new letter or word, or how to spell their own names, children ask for homework—teacher-made worksheets and "workstrips." The "big kids" do this, so our children want to do it too! In these ways, children can begin to learn to read without stress.

When children want to tell the stories of their pictures, teachers write on them what the children dictate. This leads to children making their own books—first with only a few pages, and those numbered by the teacher. The teacher reads these books to the class in Circle Time, and soon children want to learn to read them themselves.

Basic to our art curriculum have been the three mainstays—painting, clay, and collage. These three are available to the children in one form or another each week. A cooked variety of play dough which we make ourselves is particularly good for the youngest children, for whom clay is at first too hard to manage. Paint ing is done on tables with watercolors and at easels and on the floor with tempera. Finger painting is most exciting done directly on tables instead of on paper. The children can work the paint into innumerable designs before deciding which one to print. These prints made onto fingerpainting paper have made wonderful covers for books made by the children. This is a delightful project, though the clean-up is incredible! Printing of all kinds interests the children—shapes, objects from home or the classroom, numbers, letters, whatever.

We do many weaving projects and much sorting of small objects. Sewing cards, pick-up sticks, finger puppets and finger plays, string games, collages with tiny alphabet noodles, fit-together boxes, and dolls of graduated sizes are always available and are excellent tools for teaching small muscle coordination. When a Japanese mother has been available, we've tried making very elementary folded paper origami creations, and once or twice made the ravioli-like dumplings called *gyoza,* which require a lot of pinching and folding of a delightfully smooth-as-velvet dough. Although the children need a lot of help from the teacher in these projects, they love the results and concentrate long and hard on each. It is exciting to think what our children might achieve with their hands if a Japanese mother could be in the classroom with them every day. (When I taught at Nishimachi International School, I had a Japanese assistant. Fine muscle coordination was strikingly advanced in this group of mostly non-Oriental four- and five-year-olds. The art work, too, was highly sophisticated for children that age.)

An unusual project which is surprisingly popular, given its difficulty, is drawing portraits from a child model. One child sits high up on a table, and the others draw him or her. A child's uniqueness has often been astonishingly well captured by his classmates in this way. There is an atmosphere of quiet intensity when this project is in progress, and every child wants to be the model at least once, partly, no doubt, because the model takes all his pictures home—what a souvenir of his preschool days they will someday be!

Life-sized portraits are begun by tracing children lying flat on their backs. They look at themselves long and hard in the mirror before painting in the details. When all the portraits are lined up against the wall, we have a gallery of vastly different characters and personalities to enjoy, and we could use a separate exhibition space, just for these. The concentration and care required for this project are enormous for children so young, yet they take such pleasure in the result that forty-five minutes or so of painting seems worth the trouble.

In order to encourage children to use several media in the same project, we'll put out drawing, painting, and collage materials on different tables and let the children take their paper from one table to the other, adding as they go. The results are interesting, complex, and beautiful. Another activity that fascinates young children is experimenting with eyedroppers and food coloring. This is a great way to learn to mix colors: Using trays divided into twenty or thirty sections, children can mix that many shades of their original three primary colors. Box or wood-scrap sculptures can be constructed one day and painted the next. We make color wheels, books about color, and hold simple "color exhibits"—for example, of everything yellow we can find in the room. Even minimally artistic teachers can make simple but effective teaching aids for children. Often we get more ideas for making our own materials from catalogs (where the price of those tools for teaching is likely to be ridiculously high). The best reason to make your own educational equipment, however, is that it then has more personal meaning as you use it in your classroom. The more you try to make things yourself, the more willing you are to experiment with the new, an essential frame of mind for a creative teacher.

Perhaps our most exciting art projects have developed around painting murals to music. I most often use program music like *Peter and the Wolf* or *Carnival of the Animals*. But it is interesting, too, to put music on simply as a background for painting and see how art work develops differently with different music.

We approach music more directly through Eurhythmics, a system of movement to music in which rhythm first felt within the body is later translated into an understanding of musical notation. Eurhythmics was developed by Emile-Jacques Dalcroze in Switzerland. It is a particularly good complement to the Suzuki approach, which in its earliest stages does not teach note reading. Through Eurhythmics, children learn to associate a certain kind of movement with a certain kind of note (a "walking note" or a "running note"), and eventually they draw it as "a leg with a foot." Finally, the child will read notes out of a natural desire to understand what symbols stand for the movement he has felt within himself. Classes are taught around a theme and usually include the following elements: Something in response to a signal (for example, "Stop when the piano stops"); free movement in response to something (on the piano or other instrument); and children initiating a rhythm that the teacher must follow on the piano or another instrument. Children are taught to feel and understand how their own bodies relate to music, a basic and instinctual means of self-expression for any child.

Listening goes on directly and indirectly all through the Pre-School day. Recorded music may be used during Free Play or snack time, as background for an art project, or as the center of attention, as is the case with some program music. We've used Benjamin Britten's *Noye's Fludde* this way, and one child said: "When there's music and talking and singing and dancing and everything —it's an opera!" We talked about what it would take to build such a big boat, and about what an ocean is like in a storm. The watercolors painted later were extraordinary: children cared *deeply* for the music and their art work showed it.

Singing is done all the time in the Pre-School, and is one of the most important parts of our curriculum. To take an onerous edge off giving directions, we'll sometimes sing them, and children often naturally sing their reply. This is a wonderful way to relax transitions between activities and to sweeten the task of cleaning up as well. Singing to children, particularly to those who are having trouble separating from their parents, often has a remarkably calming and soothing effect. We ask parents to tell us what songs they have sung with their children at home, and we try to add those songs to our school collection. We do much group and solo singing on a daily basis and are particular about aiming for a light, unforced tone from children's voices. Many of our songs come from *Songs to Grow On,* by Beatrice Landeck, but we use many other songbooks, contributions from parents, and from the children themselves. We've taught a number of Japanese songs, and some French ones. (The more international our school, the more international our singing!) Children love to make up their own rhymes and songs—we never seem to remember to record these and the chants that we hear on the playground. But one of our Eurhythmics teachers incorporated bits of these songs into a musical play she created for the children, and they were delighted!

Math games and teaching equipment reinforce much of what is being learned in music. Concepts of time, rhythm, and counting are important to both. Direct exploration of materials has always been central to our math curriculum. Teacher-made materials are important here as in other subject areas. We can tailor math games specifically to the children if we make them ourselves. Our math equipment includes Cuisenaire Rods, inch cubes, Relationshapes, Unifix Cubes, parquetry pieces, a math balance, and cylinders of different color, height, and thickness. We have made our own lottos, books, and worksheets about number, and toys such as counting ropes, dots-to-numbers matching games, sequencing and sorting games, sandpaper numbers, and geoboards. We often count objects around the room, picking two of something from the "Mystery Box," drawing two of something and putting a circle around the "2" among other numbers on a worksheet. There are several songs we sing about number: "Two is a number . . . Two thumbs, two fingers, two hands . . . . " and others. The children learn the A string on the violin as the second string and, later, two fingers down on the A string, as "two on A."

The Cuisenaire rods have provided the children with much good exploratory play, and older children have been known to discover the relationships among them—for instance, the "staircase" of graduated lengths—without being shown. One year much interesting building had gone on with the rods before one child, obviously delighted, lined up ten white rods against one orange one and said, "They're just the same!" A special art project developed when children wanted to draw their rod constructions. Using magic markers, the children made beautiful designs. Some looked much like the constructions themselves.

As we do with letters, numbers are painted with large housepainting brushes over and over again on big rolls of paper. This is to get a feel for the direction of strokes used in making that number. Also as with letters, we draw numbers in the air for children to guess. We do number and shape collages in the same way that we do letter collages, just to familiarize children with numerals and basic shapes. We count each other, cookies, juice cups, violins, bows, and violin cases. Children never seem to grow tired of enumerating things. We may have exhibits of two of this, that, or the other. We'll gather everything we can in the room that is shaped like a triangle, or just sit in a circle, look around, and identify them. All forms of measurement intrigue the children, who are particularly interested in their height and how they grow taller. They'll climb to the top of the jungle gym and ask the teacher, "Am I taller than you *now*?"

Cooking and water play both involve much measuring and counting. In fact these activities engage children in problems of number with more concentration than almost any other projects that we do. These are as much science as math projects. Other interesting science projects are experiments with tuning forks in water and with vibration—on violin strings, from twanging taut rubber bands or tongue depressors, or feeling one's throat as one sings. We could happily do a cooking project every day and not exhaust children's interest in what is, after all, a very scientific activity. With our water table we can set up a lot of fascinating experiments concerning the properties of water in different containers and under different conditions. The color experiments with eyedroppers, food coloring, and many-sectioned plastic trays mentioned earlier are as much scientific as artistic projects. A sunny window lets us grow plants from seeds (the book *Carrot Seed* by Ruth Krauss was the inspiration for this, though our carrots never quite live up to the one in the book!).

Unfortunately, we can't keep live animals in our rented space, but each year the local nature center sends a representative with animals to our classroom. Most popular is the ferret, which fascinates the children when he turns around inside a paper towel tube. Occasionally parents have brought pets in, and it's a shame we can't have them in the school all the time. We study the human body as well. We've discussed what different senses and different parts of the body can do. We've talked about what it might be like to be without one of your senses, or perhaps to have the use of only one hand. Children are highly sensitive to those of their own age group with handicaps, and they want to talk about it.

We have a beautiful setting for nature walks. Leaf rubbings are popular in the fall; in the spring we cut buds open to see how they are made and we watch flowers burst into blossom in the class-room. We make sound cylinders out of film canisters. We may fill two with salt, two with paper clips, and leave two empty, for ex-ample, and ask the children to match the sounds. They enjoy shut-ting their eyes and guessing which sound they are hearing, which other container has the same sound, and which a different sound. We listen to sounds in the room, in the rest of the school, and out-side. We even listen to "the sound of silence." We do a lot of "Shut your eyes and . . . listen, touch, smell" or, "Remember what you saw" games. These tie in beautifully with the violin, where care-ful listening, observation, and memory are so important.

Theater games integrate movement with sense awareness and coordinate conceptual and verbal skills. These can be sug-gested by just about any other activity and complement other projects by bringing them directly to the senses. "Being" a tuning fork helps children realize what vibration is all about. "Waking Up Parts of the Body" is a game that makes them aware of one toe at a time, and "Taking a Trip" through imaginary landscapes is something children love. They ask to be balloons over and over again. Hands held in a crouched-down circle, they "blow them-selves up" very, very slowly, until they're on tiptoes, hands over their heads. Then they either "let the air out slowly" or "stick a pin in!"

A candle-making project grew out of being a melting can-dle. Some of the children really captured the feeling of the slow-ness of the melting in their movements. One child, once her body was crouched on the ground, even thought to melt out over the floor with her arms and legs. Theater games are sometimes sug-gested by the stories the children compose themselves; our Eu-rhythmics teachers have also developed musical plays out of their activities. Theater games may lead to puppet shows and then full-fledged plays. The youngest children sometimes need help getting over shyness in their first experience with puppets. They may need a teacher to suggest a few phrases that might come from a pup-pet: "Hello, how are you?" "Oh, I'm fine. What are you doing to-day?" One actress mother led the children in becoming different animals—we had been listening to *Carnival of the Animals*. She herself was so entirely unselfconscious and accurate in her por-trayal of individual animal characteristics (the distinctive arch of a lion's back and how he might stalk along through the bush) that she had the children delightedly following her lead and creating their own marvelous animal imitations. The half hour we gave her to work with the children was hardly enough. They were eager for more, and they were learning a lot about animals, too. Theater games are wonderful for developing in children a keen sense of observation and concentration as well as confidence. Children delight in the opportunity to take on new roles. I have seen otherwise shy children blossom during a theater game or play.

Integrated Learning

I have spoken a lot about integrated learning, and now I would like to give a concrete example of how various subject areas might come together to illuminate one particular skill or unit of study. Our approach to writing is generally to immerse children in the sights and sounds of language in every way we can. We read to children as much as possible, often several times a day, and we memorize a lot of rhymes and poetry together. We have been very particular about which books, rhymes, and poems we expose children to. There are books on our shelves said to be appropriate for nine- to twelve-year-olds, yet the Pre-Schoolers love them and ask for them over and over again. If children can't understand every word, they get a feeling from the story and the rhythm of its language that they can easily appreciate. Fairy tales are wonderful for very young children. The ghosts and goblins are not real, so children can be safely scared. The language of fine literature intrigues and attracts young children. Each time they hear a good story, spoken language is enhanced. Thinking progresses too, and imagination, and the development of a fine sense of humor. Children get a heightened sense of compassion and caring for others through good literature. Books that are written ostensibly for children but actually with adult concerns in mind are the ones to avoid. There are far too many such books in bookstores today, and parents might do best to depend most on what their parents read to them!

Everything experienced in violin classes encourages the coordination a child needs for writing, and play dough, clay, work with scissors, brushes, pencils, puzzles, sorting games, finger puppets, and spatial relations games are all aids to writing. A good violin bow grip is not so very far from a good pencil or brush hold. Just as we do rhythms in the air with our violin bows, we do writing in the air: "What letter is this?" We do a lot of writing on the blackboard and paint first initials very large over and over again, to make the stroke order automatic to children's hands. Games to teach the difference between left and right and to teach finger quickness and coordination are important aids to writing as well. Tracing letters in sand is also excellent practice.

At the beginning of a child's efforts to write, I cover his hand with mine and guide it through the formation of a letter over and over again. We see no point in putting off getting the feeling of the proper stroke order and motion right from the first. If we don't, we're making more trouble for the child later, when he'll have to relearn it. I'll correct a paint brush or pencil hold quickly, without saying a word, just as I would a violin bow hold, so that a child will simply *feel* the right way and learn not to be satisfied with any other.

On small cards we print words that children ask for and help them develop individual dictionaries of all the words important to them, adding to it over a whole year. These words often show up in children's first dictated stories, which they want to read and finally copy in writing. If a child wishes it, we write his own description of his painting right on it—this is the story the picture tells, in the child's own words. Early in the year we begin to make short books for children to fill. They start with separate stories on each page and advance to a story that takes a whole book to tell. The process of learning to write usually advances from their own names to other favorite words that call up strong emotions to phrases and, in some cases, whole sentences.

As part of a unit of study called "Ourselves," we took the subject of families and approached it from many different directions. This was a subject very close to the hearts of the children, and it engaged us for most of the winter term. Beginning with a scrapbook (a page for each of us with our families—teachers too), we proceeded to visits by parents presenting exciting aspects of their work to the children as a group. We did extensive drawings, paintings, and murals of whole families and individual family members (parents are always in for a few surprises during this unit).

There were innumerable counting projects (how many brothers and sisters, for example), charts made, and a fascinating discussion led by a very pregnant mother on how her baby was growing and moving inside her. This idea of the family gave rise to unprecedented amounts of story dictation and inspired attempts at writing, too. It was a time when children were most interested in asking for new words and making their own books. Full-sized self-portraits, hand prints in clay, and theater games in which children took the roles of members of their families were more ways to explore this theme. In violin class, one child said he was sorry that his father couldn't be there too: "My Daddy doesn't know how to play the violin, so I'm teaching him!"

I would like to end this chapter by describing a part of our curriculum that never was a regular event until the children made it so. One year, just before Christmas, I started playing a tape of Tchaikovsky's *The Nutcracker* during Free Play, and children began to dance to it. A very few children had had some dance lessons and a few more had seen ballet, but the way in which they took to the dance and became dancers and choreographers on a surprisingly sophisticated level was a great and happy revelation for me. "We want the *Nutcracker,* we want the *Nutcracker*!" became a daily chant, and the children's dancing developed through their own efforts into something that has often deeply moved me. You can feel the creative spirit moving in them as they dance around the room. They are careful not to let it all get silly, or to crash into one another. No teacher has ever taught them a single thing about this dancing except to suggest three rules: ballet dancers don't bump into each other, move bodies not voices, and stop when the music stops. What the children received from the teachers instead of instruction was undiluted admiration. Still, we had the feeling that they didn't really need even that, since they were off in such an exciting and imaginative world of their own. Over weeks and months, the children developed quite complex choreography and a remarkably authentic balletic approach to dancing together—girls *and* boys. (The only time some of the boys dropped out was when an older brother of one was visiting and suggested this was sissy stuff—but eventually even he joined in, when he was sure we weren't all watching him.) There is an unspoken cooperative effort among the children during this dancing, producing a beautiful rhythmic flow—a teacher's dream come true! From a birthday bouquet of flowers, I took a "wand" of silver stars on long, thin wires and put a red ribbon on it. This became a better prop for dancing even than the different swatches of colored net or scarves we had been using. To my amazement the children had a sense of how long to keep the wand, based on musical phrases, one child dancing with it until "the music said" when to pass it on to someone else. In this way it passed from hand to hand, and the whole group flowed together through sometimes half an hour of the ballet. Children were free to leave the dancing whenever they wished; often they would return. It was as if the class ran itself, or perhaps had an invisible choreographer. What is exciting to watch is how the children catch the creative spirit, getting a taste for something that transcends ordinary day-to-day existence and that will always give them pleasure. After seeing the children dance to Weber's *Spectre de la Rose,* one of our teacher-trainees wrote: "Laura appeared in the middle of the carpet for her dance solo and seemed to be completely immersed in her role as a dancer, going around and around and around—her face was transformed. I almost cried!"

CHAPTER IV

ADULTS
IN THE
CLASSROOM

The Suzuki Pre-School makes use of the skills and experiences of a wide variety of adults. First and foremost are the children's parents, who must play a very great role in their children's learning to make it successful, meaningful, and enjoyable. We also call on talented adults in and outside the community. Their visits to the school are always an enriching experience, and one that all preschools would do well to make more use of. Finally—but by no means least—are the teachers. Teaching in The Suzuki Pre-School requires continual personal growth and development. Until now our teacher training workshops have concentrated on expanding the experience of already established Suzuki music teachers to include early childhood theory and practice. In the future we plan to open the workshops to teachers without Suzuki training, who in increasing numbers have shown an exciting interest in incorporating Suzuki ideas into their regular classrooms.

Parents: Bringing Families Closer Together Through the Suzuki Philosophy

"Of all the work that people do, there is nothing more noble, nothing more important, than raising your own

child to be a fine person. . . . You bear your own children
. . . [and] the duty of bringing them up well is imposed
upon you." (Shin'ichi Suzuki, in a talk to American
mothers, *Ability Development from Age Zero*)

Why do I feel there is a new urgency in the late eighties about
establishing schools based on the Suzuki philosophy? I wish it were
not so, but the world has really become a more and more frighten-
ingly uncivilized place in which to bring up children. Adults, and
parents in particular, seem often to have lost their bearing. The
sense of moral confusion, the lack of supportive extended families, the erosion of awareness of culture and loss of articulate
expression—all have led to an impairment of parents and, through
them, their children. Confronted with the unnaturally hectic tempo of the world around them, many adults are weighed down by
a general feeling of uncomfortable foreboding and resignation in
the face of events that often seem beyond their control.

It is not only the substantive side of education, but the qualities of compassion, sensitivity, and humor that seem to have been
worn away from adults bit by bit. Where on earth did humor go?
Perhaps if adults take charge of their own lives again, they can
learn to laugh at themselves once more. Working with each other
in ways like those suggested by Dr. Suzuki might just be an important part of the solution we seek to our general befuddlement
in the last quarter of the twentieth century.

Parents, the subtlest challenge for The Suzuki Pre-School,
need to get back in touch with their own authority. They need to
be reconnected to the excitement of learning for its own sake, and
they need the confidence to set a strong example for their children. I personally wish mothers would not work outside the home
when their children are preschoolers, but we teachers simply must
accept the economic necessity of mothers out of the home as a fact
of modern life—we must work harder than ever to give parents
ways to take the richest possible advantage of the time they *do*
have with their children. Teachers must convince parents that sharing in depth with their children must become something they cannot be without. Like eating or sleeping, it is a necessary part of
every day, something one does for survival. The Pre-School, I feel,
can never do enough for parents. Since it is a gigantic commitment

we are asking of them, they may feel that too much is being asked. Yet the ultimate benefits of accomplishment and confidence are well worth it for their children.

Because parents live in this sort of world and face these sorts of problems, bringing out their potential is by far the most challenging task facing The Suzuki Pre-School—past, present, and future. This is our most difficult and most vital job, one we end each year feeling we've somehow not done well enough. It seems we could always have made ourselves clearer and always worked a little harder to encourage parents to become confidently authoritative with their children, following their own best judgment and ability as their children's most important teachers. It is the children who can remind parents how much fun it is to learn something new, and the teachers who can teach parents to teach. Yet it is also the parents who teach the teachers, by fully sharing their experiences of their own child's development.

There are enormous and unfair pressures on parents of today that militate against a centered calm, making them feel uncomfortably out of control of their lives. It is impossible (as Kenneth Kenniston said), for two adults to bring up a child in present-day America without help. We at our school are asking parents to share in depth with their children, in all areas of learning, as if those huge societal pressures didn't exist. Perhaps this is asking too much. And yet we go on asking, feeling as we do that parents must somehow seek the deepest resources in themselves, with the help of teachers, if children are to have a truly meaningful future. We need to help more of our parents find a securer identity as parents, to do their parenting thoughtfully, but not without that sense of humor so essential to the health of any human being. Parents should surely enjoy parenting—and more than most do.

It is definitely the parents we have to win to our side—over and over again. They must be given the deepest faith in themselves as teachers, because they really are more important than we who have trained in the profession, for their children. The Pre-School offers parents discussion sessions on child development and special topics, such as the controversial effect of TV on very young children, as well as workshops in as many subject areas as possible. Parents need practice, over a wide range of subjects, in teaching one learning step by approaching it from many different direc-

tions. Their goal is the same as ours: to find *the* key to that particular child's understanding. It is the same in math, science, art, and
language as it is in music and the violin, where a specific method
devised by Suzuki has influenced everything we teach.
Parents need to gain courage from our confidence in them as
uniquely imaginative teachers in their own right, according to their
own unique gifts as people. Parents who reach this degree of deep
involvement with their children are clearly rewarded, speaking
sometimes of feeling they have "a whole new and exciting life"
to share with their families.

At the same time, we must be extremely sensitive when
providing parents with workshops, discussions, and seminars, always careful to encourage them without interfering with their own
ideas about raising their children. While asking that the parents
share the child-related aspects of their lives to a considerable degree
in the interests of truly educating the whole child, we must carefully avoid letting the school become a forum for personal problems.

A typical Parents' Orientation at The Suzuki Pre-School begins with a statement which we feel is a key to the effectiveness
of the whole program: Parent commitment makes or breaks the
child's experience. Supported by that commitment, a child can succeed; without it, he cannot. Commitment then, is *crucial*. This commitment takes many forms. Parents and teachers seek the best
of both Eastern and Western cultures for children. Whenever our
own abilities are too limited, we draw on the talents of adults in
and outside the community, and we ask parents to share their interests and abilities with all the children at least once during the
year.

Our first goal for children is to *preserve* their natural delight
in learning. To assist in this, we aim to help parents remain their
children's most important teachers. We, in effect, write an individual curriculum for each child and his family, so that learning can
happen at the child's own individual pace. Learning occurs one step
at a time. Children must master each step before taking the next
one, and proper preparation by parents and teachers insures success. We try to help parents with this preparation, suggesting, for
example, activities they can share with their children outside of
school. Games with a purpose that say things a thousand different
ways (an important Suzuki-method teaching strategy at the Pre-

School) and use analogies from children's own experience give children the confidence that they need to do something really well—and the *pleasure* in the accomplishment.

Approached wisely and sensitively, children are ready to try anything and are eager to repeat that new learning endlessly, until they master it. But tired parents are too often likely to find this repetition annoying and turn if off too soon. They need to know how to "change gears" imaginatively whenever they meet their child's resistance to a new piece of learning—often, approached from another angle, this learning suddenly becomes exciting again!

At the same time, adults need to reaffirm their own joy of learning so that they will approach teaching children with energy, inventiveness, and delight. Parents can be extraordinarily good teachers of their own very young children, and the Suzuki philosophy supports this adult effort wholeheartedly.

Parents must continually think about their expectations for their children's education, as parents and teachers build that education together. Adults must be as excited about the world around them as children for The Suzuki Pre-School to succeed. As Dr. Suzuki says, every child *can* be educated to his highest potential. Parents' belief in this idea is the key to children's success and happiness.

Our challenge as teachers in this society is in asking that parents make a commitment to their children's education of a depth seldom experienced by them in any other activity in their too often frazzled day-to-day lives. In fact, parents may never before have found the time necessary to work this single-mindedly on any one thing with their children. We have to teach the joy of it! We cannot allow people to forget how to do things well, how to love deeply, and how to laugh together for the pure delight of it. This need *not* be such an extraordinarily ungracious age to live in! And TV can be reduced to the position of an occasionally amusing diversion, as it deserves to be, rather than an omnipresent "other member of the family."

We are asking parents to engage children's interests so completely in what is great about our culture and other cultures that families will experience a kind of revitalization through what they share together. When the sharing comes from self-reliance and inner resources rather than outside influences, which seem so often to be geared toward lowering people's expectations for their lives, families experience a personal strength that brings them closer together. All people respond to the joy they feel when they experience their humanity to the fullest. More than any individual curriculum, the way a teacher or parent constantly searches for new and better ways to expose children to the best of *themselves* will make or break the future. As Dr. Suzuki says, "The *authentic* needs to be instilled, so that the fake will later be rejected."

Talented Adults in the Classroom

We are totally uninhibited about asking talented adults into our classroom—from parents to Living National Treasure performers, these people provide a very special excitement in our school, and I think they get as much out of visiting very young and enthusiastic children as the children gain from exposure to them! Since we have no budget for this luxury, we are dependent upon our visitors to do "benefit performances." Some of the most talented of these people, who have often interrupted frantic schedules to give time to us, have expressed last-minute dread at the thought of facing the unknown: a group of two-, three-, and four-year olds. But once involved with the children, the richest form of sharing is their reward. Something magical happens between the generations, the excitement of sharing erases all age differences.

The late Ezra Jack Keats, a superb writer and illustrator of books for children (author of the award-winning *The Snowy Day*), had agreed to come to our class one day. Then he called me at ten-thirty the night before, his voice full of anxiety. He wanted to come because of our friendship, but though he'd written all those books for children, he didn't have the slightest idea how to deal with the children themselves—did I think he could possibly manage it? Once in the classroom, he was the hit of the year, a wonderfully warm and lovable person whom the children adoringly clung to. They not only adored but admired him as well, and he said they gave him a lot of ideas for new books he'd like to write! The children and their parents asked him to autograph their books, and some of the best pictures ever taken in the school are of Keats surrounded by what look like his own grandchildren. There is one unforgettable picture of him holding the baby sister of one of our students—he asked particularly for a copy of this. A warm and generous man, Keats was also shy and rather lonely. Later he went to Japan where a number of his books had been translated and experienced the same ecstatic welcome from mothers and children there as he did here. His was the kind of personality, like Suzuki's, that transcends cultures.

Occasionally we have had a local artist (sometimes a parent) who would spend several sessions doing his own work in the classroom. This provides tremendous inspiration for the children's art work. They don't try to copy exactly what the artist is doing, but rather respond to the feel of it and the new ideas that come from seeing another creative person at work. One record in the case study in chapter 5 is of an artist mother leading children in an art project. Here new tools are introduced, and the children's art takes a whole new and exciting direction.

A visiting sculptress from Japan, Akiko Fujita, led our children through more than an hour of sculpting an entire city of their own out of clay, using paints and simple props like toothpicks. She first put the children through a kind of Eurhythmics, a musical loosening-up session to get their bodies ready for expressive work, and then they set to sculpting: After an exciting hour of feverish activity, the children had a large part of the floor covered with their fabulous metropolis. Musicians, scientists, dancers, actors, actresses, filmmakers, mathematicians, and puppeteers have also visited our classroom. The reason for the success of this sharing is the high quality and unpatronizing manner of the presenters. Contact with the children themselves leads visitors to take this "high road" with them.

When I spent three weeks with the touring Grand Kabuki Troupe from Japan, I didn't know how much I was absorbing for my teaching and my school. Later I realized that I could bring a special visitor's gifts to the school through the learning I did outside it. The crucial element in the great success of this ninety-one-member troupe was the importance placed on working together, as hard and as well as each man could, toward the mutual goal of a top-quality performance. At every step there had to be consensus. And behind the scenes there was each man's totally secure sense of his own identity, knowing and accepting absolutely who he was. Coupled with that knowledge and acceptance were determination to excel and pride in accomplishment, each man at his own level. The troupe exuded good high spirits, sweeping us up in its infectious energy and leaving us later longing for such a feeling in our day-to-day American lives. Three weeks with the Kabuki family simply reinforced my goals for my own preschool family: that children experience learning through joy in it, and in an atmosphere as rich in sharing as in adult resources and educational materials.

I'd like to end this discussion of talented adults in the classroom with a description I wrote of an unforgettable visit to our school by members of the Bunraku Puppet Theater of Osaka, Japan. The following appeared as a contribution to the "Pre-School Column" of *The American Suzuki Journal* in the fall of 1983.

Bunraku at Suzuki Pre-School

> With a sense of special anticipation we made our way quickly through the nearly deserted Japan Society's slate gray lobby, and down the gray-carpeted stairs to the entrance to the usually off-limits dressing rooms backstage. I was to meet the visiting Bunraku Puppet Theater Troupe before tonight's opening performance. My husband Peter had been traveling with the Troupe since it arrived in Hawaii, the first of three stops on a U.S. tour that would also take them to Boston. I suddenly felt anxious as I peeked into the dressing room, and pulled back from going in— surely we were not wanted here just one hour before the opening night's performance. Before I could shy away altogether, several black-clad smiling Japanese in zoris came out to pull us into this most extraordinary self-contained small world—an efficient community of men who were engaged in repairing the wigs or costumes of puppets, checking the intricate wood and rope puppet mechanisms capable of producing on stage the effect of such a subtle variety of emotions, or tuning the twangy shamisen. This is a stringed instrument with three strings improbably made of coiled silk, which throbs insistent accompaniment to the Narrator's singing, pulling every possible ounce of emotion out of the story and the audience.
>
> Along one wall of the cramped but highly organized

dressing room, superbly crafted puppet heads perched on stands, their features in repose for only a few minutes more. The puppet mechanisms into which the heads would be fitted had been dressed in costumes and lined another wall. Before I could apologize for bursting in on this microcosm of another world, I was welcomed with overwhelming warmth: "Oku-sama, Konnichiwa!" And in not too many more minutes, I was given a delicious steaming cup of green tea in a porcelain cup. This distracted me from noticing that the chief puppeteer, Minosuke, and his assistants, Minotaro and Itcho, were assembling the puppet Osono for me to manipulate! Had I had time to start worrying about this, I never would have dared try. Instead, with little or no language exchanged between us and lots of smiles, the three took my hands into the right position on the puppet and guided me, so that the first time I tried to make her move, I was successful. What joy! What Suzuki method! (By now the *Journal* has many more readers who have visited Japan than before this summer's International Teachers Conference in Matsumoto. Those who have visited that fascinating country will perhaps have observed that the Japanese teach most everything using a kind of Suzuki method—show and do, don't talk and explain.) The feeling of holding that heavy three-foot-tall puppet and making her and her features move, is indescribable. She, Osono, seemed alive. Later we watched in awe as she was manipulated in perfectly choreographed harmony on stage by three men—two all in black with black hoods covering their faces, and one, Yoshida Minosuke III, surely a future Living National Treasure, in formal hakama. This one man's body and face expressed all the pathos of the tragic story of a woman lamenting the loss of her husband's affections. Few eyes were dry in the audience that night. In the articulate hands and through the expressive hearts of these three puppeteers, a singing Narrator—his own deep emotion felt in every sonorous and moving phrase—and the shamisen player— pulling every nuance of human emotion from those three silken strings—Osono completely devastated us, more completely than had she been human—an actress crying out with a broken heart.

After the performance we returned to that same tiny dressing room to try to express some of the feeling that was bursting from us. The Troupe was being overwhelmed by its audience—people were so moved they didn't want to leave the theater and the special mood created there that night. When the last congratulations had been graciously accepted, and the remains of the exuberant audience were finally trickling away, puppeteer Minotaro quietly drew me aside to ask me about my school. He said in Osaka the management never allows the puppets to be taken from the theater. Each one is a treasure, carved and painted by one surviving ancient craftsman. There are virtually no important disciples to carry on this unique craft. The paint used is made from crushed seashells giving a porcelain-like finish. In Japan, there could be no chances taken with the safety of the puppets, but perhaps in America where everything was freer and they weren't under the same constraints, he could fulfill a longstanding dream—to take the puppets into a classroom with very young children, something he had often wanted to do for his own child's school in Japan. Could the Troupe visit my classroom? he wondered. Could they! To think, Peter had told me in no uncertain terms this was something I absolutely must not ever ask, as much as I would want to. I am always trying to lure talented people into the Pre-School classroom, but I never dreamed my Pre-Schoolers would be exposed so directly to the excitement of such a great expression of another culture, and that it would have such a profound effect upon these children 2, 3, and 4 years old. Later one very shy child who had held a puppet was overhead saying of the puppeteer who had helped her, "He knew I wouldn't drop it." Her confidence took a great leap forward after this experience.

Some members of the Troupe spoke a little English, but the day the Japanese puppets came to the Pre-School, no language was really necessary, except the language of action expressing love and confidence in the children, reaching out to show them how to manipulate the puppets, and having the puppets interact with them as if in a play all their own. It was an extraordinary once-in-a-lifetime experience for mothers, teachers, and children. At first there was a shyness toward the visitors, but that was soon dispelled by the puppets. Most memorable was a "dialogue" between a five-month-old baby and the Osono puppet, the two "chatting and smiling" together so happily that the baby cried when the puppet finally had to "say goodbye." Puppets and children reached out to each other, bringing tears to many eyes. Japan and America reached out to each other too, more surely than at any international conference of diplomats politely bowing to one another.

Reverberations of that day were felt in the Pre-School long afterward. The children drew their impressions of the puppets, which were sent to Japan with the Troupe, and learned that their pictures had been shared with Japanese children of the same age in the school Minotaro's child attends. The Japanese mothers were apparently struck by the very different color sense of American children. Our Pre-Schoolers abundantly understood that day that they were experiencing something very special—what we would call being in the presence of true greatness. The children's attention span was stretched way beyond its usual limits and there existed absolutely no barrier between cultures, in that atmosphere where their ability to understand and appreciate what was being presented to them was fully respected. For the rest of the year the Japanese puppets and the men who manipulated them came into the children's work and play often—puppets were made, puppet shows were given with new inspiration, and every child's eyes eagerly devoured the excellent photographs of the Bunraku visit, which tell more than this narrative ever could.

Teacher Training

Perhaps the most exciting long-term development in our school has been the advent of teacher training. In June of 1983 we gave our first five-day teachers' workshop: "Introduction to The

Suzuki Pre-School," and it has become a last-week-of-school tradition ever since. This is by far the best way we have of encouraging the development of other such schools. The workshop stresses the importance of a true sense of the *spirit* of Suzuki teaching, while exposing its participants in depth to the method.

At the workshop orientation meeting, we always tell teachers that observation of the children themselves during this week will be the most important piece of learning they'll do with us. We ask them to do that observing in a sensitive way, to "feel their way," making themselves "a part of the woodwork" until children are ready to bring them into their activities. We advise them not to "do for" the children, but rather watch how children approach projects themselves. In lieu of taking notes, which might be distracting, we suggest making mental notes on one child, following his activities and development particularly closely through the five days. We tell teachers that what they will see during this brief period will be not a typical week, but a potpourri of projects from the whole past year.

The workshop is set up for morning observation and afternoon seminars and workshops. We follow our usual morning schedule, with changes made for special visitors (an older child performing on the violin from the afternoon school, a demonstration by a Suzuki cello teacher and her son in which our children delightedly participate, or, one year, an Orff class). In the afternoon we present sessions on Suzuki and other important educational thinkers, the curriculum of the Pre-School, and teaching violin to young children and their parents. Additional specialists in different years have given workshops in math, science, Orff for Suzuki Teachers, Special Education, and Eurhythmics. One opportunity is given teachers each workshop to work with Pre-School materials and educational equipment, at their own learning level, with or without the children. We ask teachers to observe music-school teaching and note how Pre-School ideas tend to enrich teaching there—both the substance of the teaching and the teachers' sense of the importance of early childhood development. We also make a special effort to show the teachers how the work of the Pre-School has been influenced by Japan and its culture. We suggest to teachers the background Suzuki is coming from by showing one of a number of films on Japanese life at a special dinner given near the end of the week. In our school, that country's inspiration influences more than the violin work alone. The Japanese approach to teaching and parenting has had a great impact on my thinking and teaching. We are a different culture, with our own strengths, but it is interesting that Japan may have some important answers for our greatest and most unnecessary weaknesses: lack of ability to work together, resignation to and acceptance of a state of increasing mediocrity ruling our lives, and lack of centeredness in whatever we do. Japanese parents are also, on the whole, spectacularly good at communicating to their children their own pleasure at being parents, and the generations seem to have such fun together!

Comments from past participants in the workshop have been inspiring, and some have strongly suggested that this kind of training should be extended to educators beyond the field of music, noting that the program had much to offer to all educators in early childhood development. Responses such as these have led us to our next move, to include in our teacher training teachers not trained in Suzuki techniques or even especially in music. For some time now we have hoped to start a long-term teacher training program over a whole year. Unfortunately not many teachers can fit their schedules to this plan, and those interested often seem to live either out of state or out of the country. Until we can inaugurate this more in-depth training for teachers interested in the work of our school, we'll continue to train new people on the job, wherever and whenever possible. I think the long-term project would be easier to set up in a college or university, where the Pre-School could act as a lab school for teacher training. We could train college students to be teachers through direct Pre-School experience in the mornings, and teach seminars and workshops in the afternoons or evenings.

A long-term teacher training program would focus on developing a comprehensive curriculum directly inspired by the Suzuki philosophy. What it would *not* be is a nursery through sixth grade early childhood course, better taught in an education school. A central concern would be to give teacher trainees an introduction to Suzuki ideas through all the subject areas covered in the Pre-School. Feeling that Pre-School ideas can easily be carried into music studios and non-Suzuki early childhood classrooms, we would also expose students to the best of non-Suzuki educational thinking, as it fits remarkably with the Suzuki approach. Our aim would be to bring Suzuki thinking into the mainstream of current educational thought—a force to be reckoned with and an idea that does not come and go like an educational fad. This would be our best forum for expressing our feeling that the Suzuki philosophy offers imaginative and practical solutions to many problems this country now faces in educating its children.

In the teacher training program that we envisage, we will use the violin, because that is what we know. But there is absolutely no reason why other instruments could not be equally good centerpieces for such a preschool program. We have long thought the Pre-School might be the perfect place to start a school-wide cello program.

We would offer a thirty-two-week session in which teachers would spend as many mornings as they could spare in the Pre-School, observing and gradually doing more and more of their own teaching. Afternoons and evenings would be spent in seminars and workshops and in observing music school teaching, upon which the Pre-School has been based.

Observation and recording of the learning patterns and development of individual children would be required, culminating in a final study in depth of one child due at the end of the year. We would provide at least one session on the practical and legal aspects of running one's own school, and another on the challenges of creative fund-raising at a time when all non-profit institutions are "going begging" and sources of funding are severely limited. Each teacher trainee would be responsible for creating an original unit of instruction and teaching it in the classroom, with other trainees observing and submitting comments. Discussions with talented professionals who have visited the classroom and parents who have worked with us would be arranged. "Hands-on" workshops in each subject area would be taught as if to preschool children, so that teachers would get a feel for this kind of curriculum development and for the flexibility and creative thinking necessary within it.

To know how to maintain children's inborn eagerness and

enthusiasm for learning is to listen carefully to the lessons they teach us as we observe them in depth. Just as we have developed farthest as teachers through observation of other teaching and of children learning, we feel we have a rare and exciting opportunity here to extend Dr. Suzuki's ideas beyond music, and even the limitations of our own school—through teacher training.

A CASE STUDY: ONE CHILD'S STORY IN THE SUZUKI PRE-SCHOOL

T his study was done as one of the requirements for a master's degree at Bank Street College of Education. Although it reflects a specific child in a specific setting at a specific time, I believe it gives a feeling for the atmosphere of our school, and that lessons drawn from it can be more generally applied.

There was little time to observe all the children in the class in depth before a decision had to be made as to which child I would use for the case study. J.G. arrived at the orientation meeting on September 25, and immediately I noticed interesting changes in her behavior since I had seen her last in May. I saw her assuming a very different position in relation to the group, and I wanted to pursue that further.

J. was four in mid-December. She is physically very attractive, having an unusually expressive face—rounded but not plump, with wide sparkling eyes and a mobility of features that would find good use in the theater. She seems to us to be a miniature of the adult she will become. We speculate she will be very like her lively, attractive mother. J. has an unusual range of facial expressions for an equally wide range of emotions. She is well-proportioned and moves fluidly, with good coordination and grace.

She has excellent health. In general, her physical well-being and extremely likable, outgoing personality seem to draw people to her. In September, she weighed thirty-three pounds and was thirty-seven and one-half inches tall. Her voice seems more mature than those of the other children. It is slightly high-pitched but not in any way babyish. She uses her voice like an actress, yet she seems perfectly natural and unselfconscious.

There are usually six children in our group, of whom J.G. is the oldest. Two are boys and four are girls. The age range is from three years and two months (A.J.) to four years and one month (J.G.). There are always two adults present, with a third teaching Eurhythmics in a room upstairs. One day a week all the parents stay to share the children's experiences with them and, particularly, to learn enough violin technique to help their children at home. The overall personality of the group of children, now that they are used to being separated from their parents, is one of purposeful activity and enthusiasm. It is a lively collection of individualists—characters every one.

Each child spends two and one-half hours at school, three days a week. There is no lunch provided, only a snack of juice, crackers, and cookies. No rest period is necessary. The children come largely from the Upper West Side of Manhattan, with one exception (A.J.). We began the year with two children from my town, Hastings, but they had to drop out except for occasional visits because of the mother's difficulty with a new pregnancy and the strain of the trip on her son, who won't be three until March. We enjoyed having his sister, M., come along. An older child was an inspiration to the younger ones. The mother was also a great help to us, doing art projects with the children which were far more ambitious than the ones we can do on our own. Except for one child (A.O.), all come to school with their parents and go home with them, too.

J.G.'s parents are separated. J.'s mother, combining practicality and a sense of humor, is doing an unusually good job, we think, of keeping J.'s life as normal and full as if the father were home. He visits the home often, and at least once brought J. (very late) to school, laden with gifts after an outing they had shared. J.'s mother is determined not to undermine the father's image in front of J., but privately seems worried about his effect on her.

J.G.'s mother tells us that J. is full of curiosity about everything around her, at home as she is at school. She and J. read together constantly and enjoy long conversations together. Mrs. G. makes a point of giving J. as much information about the world as she asks for. J. takes an idea started at school and develops it further at home. (After the clay project of October 8, J. made a "fish pond" of clay and little clay fishes to go in it. She tried putting water in it right away and observed, "You have to let it dry or it will leak.") She makes up rhymes, chants, and songs, and is basically a cheerful, spirited creature.

J's past schooling was with us last year. She contributed much less to the group last year than this year. She was hardly a leader then (there were other children older than she), and she was quick to pout if she didn't get her way immediately. She shied away from trying anything new that she thought was going to be hard for her. Not only was she younger, but she was also going through the worst shock of her parents' separation. That has clearly been the biggest stress on J.'s life so far. This year both mother and child seem to be much less affected by it (or more resigned to it), though, and somehow things are on a more even keel. J. adores her father, frequently saying, "My Daddy gave me this!" (during Show and Tell), or "That's my Daddy!"—the biggest, strongest thing in an often black drawing or painting. Though we teachers have not visited J.'s home, J. and her mother visited the home of the other teacher to see her new baby. J. was apparently very shy and totally enthralled, talking about it in a hushed voice afterward. Mrs. G. seems to us to have done a wonderful job putting J.'s interests before her own emotions in this difficult time for both of them. She seems to thoroughly enjoy bringing J. up and shares a great deal in a very warm way with her child.

Record: Getting Ready for Outdoor Play (October 1, 1975)

The teacher had just finished reading a second story, *The Carrot Seed,* during which J.G. had participated a lot, saying how delicious she thought carrots were and guessing the ending through all the pages when the carrot wouldn't grow: "It'll grow in the end!" she said over and over, with just a tinge of doubt in her voice. The teacher noticed the clock and said, "Okay, it's time to line up to go out. Remember to be very quiet in the halls." J.G. rushed pell-mell to the head of the line, nearly knocking down unsuspecting S.P., who had stood up and just happened to be first, apparently not dreaming of the possibilities for fierce competition for first place in line. The teacher told J.G. she could see S.P. didn't like to be pushed out of the way, and said, "You can get behind him, J." J.G.'s mobile and expressive face went into a sad-eyed pout and she hung her head down. Then she dragged her feet to a point just barely behind S.P. Suddenly, her eyes had turned angry-hurt and her body had the look of a cat about to spring. As the teacher turned her back and started up the stairs, a scuffling sound and cries of indignation made her turn around. There was J.G. right behind her, a face full of triumph and defiance. "See, I *am* the leader!" S.P. seemed to have had enough by now and tried to push J.G. back. M.C. shouted, "You are NOT the leader!" and the teacher said, "It doesn't matter who is first. You were first yesterday, and maybe you can be the leader some other day." The teacher barely heard J.G. as she said, "But I like to be next to you!" and furiously stomped her way back to the room, where she threw herself face down onto the rug in the reading corner. The teacher sat down next to her and waited until J. turned her head just enough to peek at the teacher out of the corner of her eye. The teacher held out her hand and said, "Come on, J., everyone's waiting for you." As J.G. walked back to the other children holding the teacher's hand, she gave the teacher an on-again, off-again smile. The rest of the class watched her somewhat warily as J.G., now all smiles, joined the end of the line.

Record: Working with Clay (October 8, 1975)

B., a mother in our group who helps us with art projects, set up this afternoon's work with clay for all the children so that I could record the session. (Usually I would be teaching half the class violin while B. took the other half for art.) The other teacher was thus also able to share in the art project. B. had set up one cookie sheet for each child on which were a mound of potter's clay, homemade "tools" for working, and a seashell. Each child's mother was encouraged to participate in the background, as the children worked at the tables with B. The children sat at two tables pulled together, eight around the "circle."

B.'s son, C., was the first to ask, "What's the shell for?" B. said to the whole group, "Have you ever been to the beach before, and did you feel how sticky the wet sand was? Well, that's what they make clay out of." J.G., noticing a tool she hadn't gotten on her cookie sheet said, "I want one of those too!" B. was waiting for the children to finish their questions before she answered the question about the shells. J.G. began right away to roll her clay into snakelike shapes, each time pulling off quite a small amount from the larger mound. She then began making balls and said, "I'm making it to a ball!" and later, "I have a ball already!" spoken to no one in particular. Her approach so far had been delight tempered with timidity and curiosity. With eyes wide and mouth a little bit open she worked on her ball to press it flat down on the cookie sheet. B. saw her chance to explain the shells, and said, "Pick up your shells and feel them." Her daughter M., who is almost five and comes to school because she cannot be left alone at home, has proved to be very good with the younger children and an inspiration to them. J.G., clearly enthralled by M., stared at her as she said, "The shell is smooth just like the clay." B. said, "You can make it rough or smooth just like the shell, with the tools or your finger." J.G. was making tiny pinches in a small part of her clay, then flattening them down. B. introduced pieces of wire to anyone who wanted to try using them. C. immediately said he wanted some. J.G. was emphatically not ready, and said loudly, "I don't want any, I'm still working." Then she looked around the group and announced, "I used to have a clay set!" When nobody paid any attention because they were all so absorbed, she repeated that statement, waited for a reaction, got none, and matter-of-factly went back to work. Now she said, "I'll try some," meaning the wire. J.G. watched B. showing another child how to use the wire and tried it herself. At the moment the wire cut through the clay, J.G.'s face broke into a wide-eyed, unbelieving smile. She said, triumphantly, "Hey, I got one piece, I did it!" With that piece she used the flat of her hand and soon said, "Hey, I'm making a pancake!"

Generally J.G. was using small bits of clay and working with them separately, not putting them together. She noticed C., across from her, sticking toothpicks into his clay, and she watched with mouth hanging open, eyes wide. M., sitting next to J.G. (by J.G.'s choice), said, "I made a baby porcupine!" and showed the whole class her ball of clay with toothpicks sticking out of it and a smiling face scratched on one side. J.G. intently watched M.'s every move. Looking at one of her own early snake-like pieces of rolled clay, J. said, "I don't want to make a tail," and seconds later, "I'm making a baby porcupine!" She was rolling the ball for the body while she watched M., not yet adding toothpicks. Then she began to add toothpicks, looking all around the class to see what the others were doing as she did so.

B. then introduced a garlic press and a sieve for making new shapes with the clay and showed the children how to use them. Immediately after B. first used the words "garlic press," J.G. said, "I want a garlic press!" B. let J.G. use the press first. As J.G., using both hands to squeeze the clay through, first saw the hair-like stringy clay results pushing through the press, her face was completely wreathed in smiles. It probably wouldn't be possible for J.G.'s expressive wide-eyed face to show any more delight and surprise. J.G. became totally absorbed in picking the "hairs" off the press and trying to put them on a ball of clay she had rolled before. Impatient with the difficulty of that, she sighed, "Oh well," and squooshed the "hairs" right into the ball.

Other children were having a try at the press when B.P. (age three), sitting on the other side of J., grabbed some clay from an unsuspecting A.J. on his other side, and announced, "I want that garlic press!" B. comforted a distraught A.J. and told B.P. he could ask her for more any time. J.G. said to B.P., "See, you don't have to be a bad boy!" Then she said, "I want that thing again, too!" Just then M. announced, "Hey, look what I made, a little Raggedy Andy!"

B. asked J.G. if she'd had another chance with the garlic press and J.G., in her excitement, said, "No, I didn't do it myself again a bit!" Just then B.P. grabbed another hunk of A.J.'s clay and J.G. responded immediately: "Don't take her clay and don't take mine, either!" J.G. went back to work now, picking up the "hairs" one at a time, and putting them on the ball. Suddenly she looked up and said, "When mine is dry, I'm going to paint it." J. now got a turn at the sieve and added some sieve "hair" to the ball. Other children were finishing up, taking off their smocks and putting their finished clay pieces on paper plates B. had provided for drying. J.G. kept on working laboriously at the difficult-for-her job of putting the hairs on the ball. She tried to scratch a face into the ball and said, "See, that little girl's looking down at something and she's getting scared. She's getting more hair and more hair!" C. said, "J. is my favorite!"

Only the sounds of snack being prepared pulled J. away from the clay.

Record: Reaction of Child and Whole Class to First Music Listening Experience —*Danse Macabre* (October 28, 1975)

The teacher put the class in the mood for the recording by very briefly describing the story behind the music. She told the children to listen for the clock striking midnight ("Count the strokes"), the ghosts slowly coming out to dance on Halloween night, the ghosts dancing faster and faster, the rooster crowing ("Halloween is over and they can't dance again until next Halloween"), and finally the sound of sad ghosts and skeletons slinking away as the sun comes up.

J.G. said "Oooh!" when she heard what the story was about and plumped face-down on the floor. B.P. followed, putting his body as close to hers as possible. They turned their faces toward each other and grinned, as they waited for the music to begin. S.P. looked a little embarrassed at this and stayed sitting on the floor looking at the record player with some apprehension. A.O. stood by the machine and watched every move as the teacher put the needle on the record. The clock in the music began striking and the teacher was counting the strokes. The children seemed delighted and somewhat awed that the striking of midnight really was happening on the record as promised, and began to join the counting.

J.G. was the first to hear the sound of ghosts beginning their dance, and she whispered in a frightened but thrilled voice: "The ghosts are coming!" S.P. echoed this with, "The ghosts," and B.P. pulled himself even closer to J.G., all the while grinning uncertainly. L.Z. opened her eyes wide, staring at the record player, and got up to her feet to do a turn to the music, grin self-consciously, and sit down again. A.J. skipped in a wider circle around the room, then came back to lie down next to B.P. When the teacher pointed out the sound of the skeletons rattling. S.P. said, in a rather high-pitched, excited voice, "Oooooh . . . the skelingtons!" A.O. was the only child not wrapped up in the music. She had stopped enjoying and started worrying when she heard the word "ghosts." (Afterwards the whole class talked about real and "just pretend," but it wasn't clear even then that A.O. understood.)

As the music gathered momentum, the teacher didn't need to give any further explanation. J.G. said, "Fasterandfasterand-FASTER!" as if she didn't have time to pause between words. S.P. and B.P. echoed this with "Faster!" and then looked surprised that they'd said it at the same time. A.J. began moving her arms like branches swaying in the wind when the teacher said, "Listen to the wind howling, louder and softer and louder again!" L.Z. followed her in this with a smile on her face. A.O. continued to sit watching the whole proceeding with some suspicion.

As the music was swirling toward its climax, J.G. got up and danced along. A.O. looked as if she'd like to join but didn't, and A.J. said, "Faster and faster and louder and louder!" The teacher then told them to listen pretty carefully for the sound of the rooster crowing—it would be quite soft. When it came, J.G. looked as if she was about to burst with pleasure: "I heard it, I heard it!" S.P. and B.P. were straining to hear the crowing, and A.O. went over to the machine as if to find the rooster itself there. All the children seemed moved when they heard the mournful sounds of the end of the dancing for this Halloween, and their faces showed genuine regret. "They have to wait all until next year," said J.G. with a sigh and a good deal of sadness in her voice. When the record had finally stopped (A.O. watching the whole mechanical workings with fascination), the children were all quiet for a moment. Then J.G. said, "I like that ghost song. Play it again!"

Record: Observation of a Child during Eurhythmics (December 4, 1975)

J.G. and the other children are clustered on the floor around the Eurhythmics teacher, who is drawing characters from a story she is telling and accompanying with music. The children are mainly sitting up with heads tilted forward so as not to miss any stroke of the teacher's magic markers as they make figures appear as if by magic.

TEACHER (*as she almost completes one lively drawing*) What's this?
S.P. (*delighted at the recognition*) A Jack-in-the-Box!
TEACHER We'd better make him a smiling Jack-in-the-Box. .
J.G. (*staring at the picture, mouth partly open and body straining to get closer to the paper*) Give him eyes!
TEACHER (*giving the Jack-in-the-Box eyes, looks at the finished drawing and then gets up on her feet and back down on her haunches*) Can you get in your boxes? (*The children all crouch down and she says suddenly*) Jack . . . jump! (*All jump up to more than their full height, as if they were on springs*)
J.G. (*with eyes wide*) My neck really got strained! (*Folds herself back into crouched in-the-box position*)
TEACHER Okay, everybody in your box! (*Some grinning children pretend they can't fold themselves back up into their boxes. They giggle as the teacher pushes them back down.Continuing the story*) What other toys did Santa pack? Here's a spinning top. (*Drawing the motion lines as well as the top itself*) It's going round and round. What happens when it stops?

J.G. and B.P. get up and spin around the room once to demonstrate. The teacher moves to the piano and plays music of ever-decreasing speed. J.G. and B.P. and now all the children pick up the tempo of the top as it spins slower and slower. J.G. has an expression of contentment on her face, seeming to delight in every minute of this. Her body moves rhythmically to the music and tries to fit itself to the changes in tempo. When the piano stops, all fall down giggling, the teacher enjoying it as much as the children. They beg to repeat this and do.

J.G. (*having forgotten to turn around and spin the other way for a change, as the teacher had suggested*) The world's going around!
TEACHER (*catching J.G., whose dizziness has made her quite tipsy*) Spin the other way!

Meanwhile A.J., who has a cold and is just back from an absence, is looking all around, especially at us observers. She is not participating now, and held the teacher's hand as she came upstairs. When she does join in she looks over at us to see our reaction. Now she has walked back to us, and in the middle of all this spinning top activity, tells us with shining eyes and a sense of something private shared just among us three: "I saw Santa."

The teacher is now drawing a train and appointing J.G. the first conductor, for a new song with movement, one the teacher has made up for the children, *Clickety Clack.* To a very catchy tune that captures the feeling of a train moving faster and faster, then slowing down and finally stopping, it goes: "Clickety Clack, Clickety Clack, Running down the railroad track. Clickety Clack, Clickety Clack, Whoo . . oo, Whoo . . oo."

J.G. eyes the picture of the train with what looks like longing: "Is that one for me to take home?" Each day that the teacher has done this kind of illustrated story-telling, J.G. has wanted to take all the pictures home. (At the end of the class the teacher gave each child a picture.)

J.G. takes her place as the "engine." Each child puts his hands on the shoulders of the child ahead and the train begins to move to the piano accompaniment. Only A.J. is not joining in. She looks toward us for direction and we encourage her to join. She does, but only later when we are not watching. A.J.'s movements are a little babyish compared to the others, but she is happily with them at last. Her legs move in abrupt large movements too big to fit the rhythm. As the children move up from being caboose to engine, A.J., who started on the end, gets her turn to lead. She grins and flails her arms out to her sides as she galumphs around the room, looking pleased but far from unselfconscious. When B.P. leads the train, he has trouble pulling the whole group along, so he breaks free, following the piano rhythm around and around the room, limbs swinging freely and body fitting the music well.

When S.P. is the engine, he gets a hesitant, slow start. Then his mouth opens into a wide smile, and off he goes. Soon he also detaches himself from the train and swoops around in wide circles, not stopping until the music is long over. There is a gleam in his eyes. When A.O. leads again, the momentum of the train ride is really over and the children break apart. All move in their own style, not particularly to the music. A.J. by now is back with us, not wanting to join in. "I think A. is waiting at the station," says the teacher. A.O., who has been most shy of all about being the engine, now breaks free, moving in very rhythmic circles around the room, with a totally relaxed body and a huge smile on her face.

Record: Observation of a Child During Show and Tell (December 9, 1975)

J.G. has a pot in each hand, one with a plant she's brought from home and another with dirt in it. She's standing near the window, and the other children are looking curiously at what she's brought.

TEACHER Come on over here and bring your plant, J.

J.G. (*coming to the reading corner where Show and Tell is usually held and plopping down on a pillow, pots miraculously still in each hand. She is very satisfied looking*) Well . . . see . . .

A.J. (*interrupting, in a whining voice*) I don't have anything.

(*The teacher helps J. set the two pots on the floor, and J. begins to dig into the dirt in the second pot with the spoon she has brought from home.*)

J.G. (*some of the dirt spills out*) Oops! Have to make a hole . . .

TEACHER What do you put in the hole, J.?

J.G. A seed! (*Puts the seed very carefully down in the hole. Other children show great interest. Some have mouths open and all are peering into the hole to see the seed*) Now cover it up . . . . (*J.G. seems very proprietary*) Now I'll go get some water . . . (*All eyes follow her as she goes out of the room. At this moment she has complete control over the situation, but is so engrossed she doesn't seem to be aware of it*)

B.P. What do you put water in for?

TEACHER Why do you think you put water in it, B.? (*When B.P. simply looks puzzled, the teacher asks S.P. the same question*) Do you remember the carrot seed in the story S.P.? (*S.P.'s favorite story*) Why do you need water?

S.P. (*very pleased with himself*) Then it will grow. (*J.G. returns, and all are eagerly watching her. B.P. has watched the door for her return, and looks happy when he sees her*)

J.G. (*pouring water ever so slowly*) Very carefully you do it. (*Giving the teacher the pot with the seed and keeping the one with the plant*

in it) This plant's for you. I think I'll put it over here, right
here.(*Puts it on the windowsill next to our geranium*) This plant's
for home for me. (*Puts the pot with the tiny green leaves on the
mantle, with the teacher's help*)

TEACHER Can we keep our plant here and let all the children water
it, J.?

J.G. (*smacking her lips with satisfaction* Yes, every morning water
it. And keep it in the sun! (*Said with a warning gesture of a finger.
J.G. goes out to get more water, and the teacher brings the leafy plant
back in the circle so the children can see*)

B.P.She's getting some more. . . .

TEACHER Yes, some more water. (*When J. returns*) A., how much
does she have to put in? (*A. just stares at the plant*)

S.P. (*said in a quiet, rather awed tone*) Tiny.

J.G.Then I'll put it in the ground.

TEACHER Then what do you think will happen?

J.G. It'll grow up!

TEACHER Do you think it will look like this plant? Do you know
what kind of plant it is?

J.G. No, do you know?

TEACHER No, I don't. But I think maybe it's just like the one you
are taking home.

A.J. (*impatiently, hardly waiting for the teacher's last words*) Now
it's my turn!

Record: Observation of Children Making Candles (December 10, 1975)

Feeling that the children should have the experience of candle making with chopped ice, the teacher made some concessions to
safety. She poured the hot wax and broke up the ice with the children's help, putting the ice in a plastic bag and smashing it with
a hammer. The children positioned the plain candle (an easier way
to get a wick than trying to hold the string in the ice) in the chopped
ice in the milk carton (cut down to about four-inch height). This
was mostly an observation lesson in science and led to all sorts
of other projects concerned with language, math, and other
subjects.

As the children came into the room from Eurhythmics, they

first noticed the large pot on the stove, with two coffee cans of hot clear wax sitting in boiling water. We put the children up on a table so they could see and asked them to hand us pieces of crayon (red or green) which were to make the colors for the candles.

J.G. Wow, lookit! The water is bubbling!

S.P. Why the cans move?

TEACHER The water is so hot it is boiling and that makes the cans dance in the water.

B.P. I want to put red crayons in. (*The teacher gives him one and he carefully lets it fall into the hot, clear paraffin*)

J.G. I want green. (*The teacher gives her a green crayon, and she watches it begin to melt—eyes wide, mouth open*)

A.J. I want green too.

She is afraid to go near the hot wax, so the teacher helps her put her crayon in. The teacher adds more crayons to the red and green pots, about five crayons each, to get a good color. The children seem surprised when all the crayons are melted.

J.G. They're all gone!

TEACHER Yes, J., the crayons melted because it was so hot in the wax.

J.G. Just like the snowball in Peter's pocket? (*We had just read* A Snowy Day, *by Ezra Jack Keats*)

TEACHER Yes, J., except that snowball melted more slowly. Peter's house wasn't this hot, it was only warm.

B.P. (*very excited, he jumps up and down on the table*) Lookit! The pots are really jumping now!

S.P. (*also very excited*) Is it ready now?

, TEACHER Let's get the ice ready.

She gets the children off the table and they all stand around looking at the ice in trays, a hammer, a plastic bag and some twistums as she brings them to the table. She holds the bags while the children put the ice cubes in and helps them tie the twistums. Then she takes the hammer and shows how to hit the bags so the ice will break up.

B.P. Let me try that. (*He takes the hammer and, teacher's hand lightly on his, hits the ice fairly gently*)

TEACHER You can hit it a little harder than that, B. (*She shows him and then lets him try it alone. He hits harder and the ice breaks up more to the desired size*)

S.P. and J.G. Let me try, let me try! (*Only A.J. doesn't want a try*)

TEACHER Now, put your candles into your milk cartons and S. and I will pour the chopped ice in around them. (*The teachers do this and find it's hard for the children to hold the candle in the middle with the ice coming in around it. But with help, this is accomplished*) Now we are ready to pour in the hot wax. What color do you want? (*Only B.P. wanted red*) You have to be very careful now. S. is going to pour the hot wax. You must stand away. The hot wax could give you a burn. (*Each child stands far enough away for safety and watches his carton being filled with colored wax. Almost immediately the ice makes some of the wax harden*)

S.P. Look, the candle is drying!

TEACHER When the hot wax hits the cold ice, what do you think happens?

J.G. It gets hard.

TEACHER Yes, J., and do you know what will happen to all that ice?

J.G. (*eyes wide, mouth open*) No, what?

S.P. It will melt!

TEACHER That's right, S. (*S.P. wants to touch it*) Don't touch it yet. It's still too hot. (*By now the candles are hardening enough so that it's possible to feel the hardness through the cartons*) Try to hold your carton very gently. See if it's getting hard.

J.G. Mine is!

S.P. Mine also!

A.J. I want to take mine out.

TEACHER We have to wait until they are all hard and cold. Let's put them on a tray and take them downstairs to get really hard. Then you can take them home.

J.G. That's magic!

B.P. Yeah.

S.P. It's a Christmas candle.

A.J. It's for my Mommy.

Record: Observation of Children During Theater Game: Melting Candles (December 10, 1975)

TEACHER Everybody stand up really tall and straight. (*Shows stiff*

Teacher Marai Yaw reading to students.

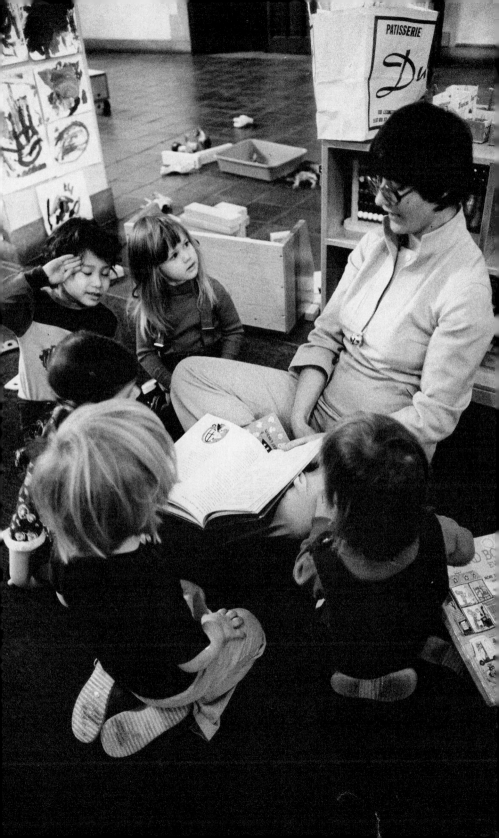

Working on a puzzle together.

Facing Page: Busy with watercolors. Above: Drawing by a four-year old at The Suzuki Pre-School.

Author and illustrator of children's books Ezra Jack Keats autographing books for Suzuki Pre-School students.

Top left: Classroom at The Day School. Bottom left: Painting at the easel. Above: Exploring a math balance.

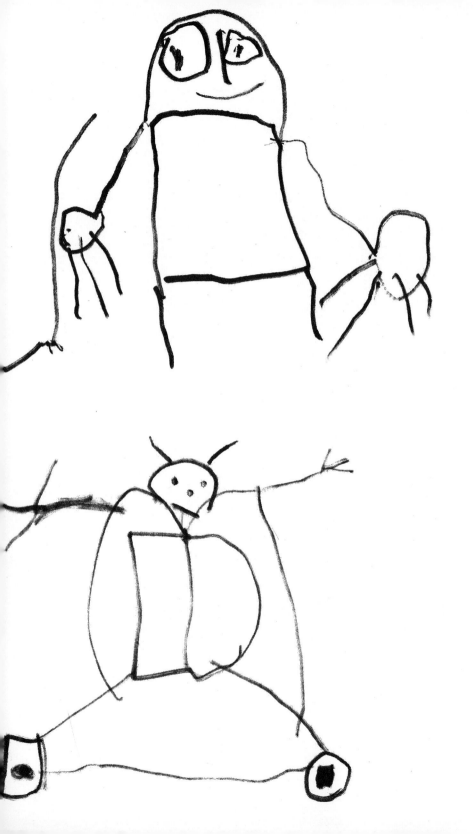

Drawings by Suzuki Pre-
Schoolers.

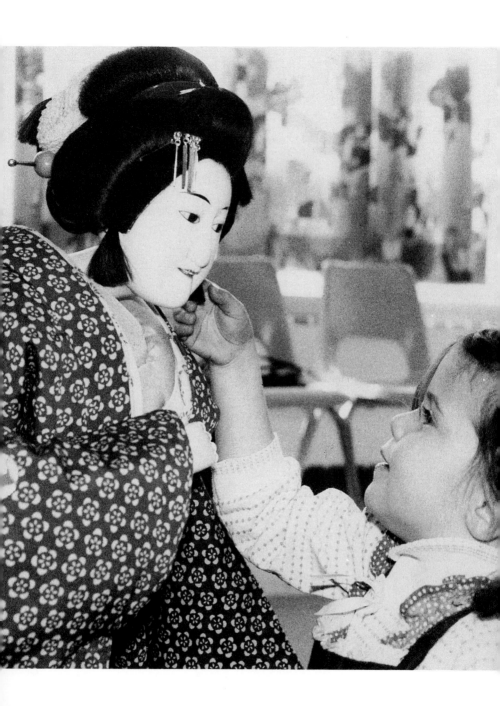

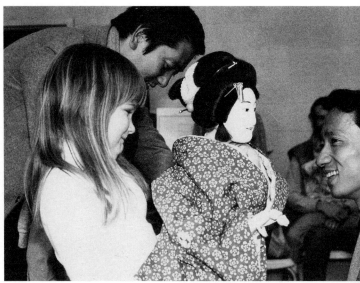

Bunraku at The Suzuki Pre-School, with narrator Rodayu
and puppeteer Minotaro.

Page 142, top: Teacher Nancy Dexter singing with children. Page 142, bottom, and page 143, top: Suzuki Pre-School students perform their musical play *The Enormous Turnip*. Page 143, bottom: Susan Grilli reading to students.

posture, with arms straight down at sides. The children stand not only stiffly, but hold their breaths)

S.P. *(gets up on tiptoe)* See, I am tall.

TEACHER Now stand very still. I am going to come around and light each candle. *(She takes a pretend match, strikes it, and walks around the circle touching each child on the head. S.P. grins, almost grimaces when she does this to him)* Now you are beginning to burn, and slowly, very slowly you will begin to melt. *(She tilts her head slowly to the right and lets her knees begin to bend)*

J.G. *(who had melted very fast and lay on a heap on the floor)* See, I'm all gone!

A.J. and A.O. are having trouble making their knees bend slowly enough. A.J. flops suddenly and A.O. follows her example, grinning. S.P. has the longest "melt" of all. When he finally touches the floor he lets out a sigh and smiles.

J.G. I like that!

B.P. Do it again!

TEACHER Okay, let's do it again. Stand up very straight and stiff. Now I'll light all the candles. I'm beginning to melt!

S.P. *(swaying back and forth and grinning this time, looking all around at the other children and at the teacher)* See, I'm not melting. I'm not melting this time!

J.G. I melted all the way down. *(She had gone down slower this time and had even spread her arms out on the floor "melting" along the ground too)*

TEACHER When you light your candles, see if they melt the way you did!

Record: Observation of Children in the Doll Corner (December 11, 1975)

S.P. *(said to the teacher who then moves off)* I'm fixing up the babies —playing house!

J.G. *(making mouse-like noises, apparently instructions to S.P. I am too far off to hear much of it, and it is difficult to understand anyway, with voices pitched so high)* Can I please? Let me just feel it. Let me just look at it. *(S. lets her touch baby in doll house)* What are you making for supper?

Dr. Suzuki waving goodbye to participants at the Manhattan School of Music Workshop, April 1978.

S.P. (*very matter-of-fact*) I'll fix dinner.

J.G. I'll clean up the house.

S.P. The babies are sleeping. I'm going over here. (*Goes to house-keeping area where dolls are bigger and where there is cooking equipment. He puts an artichoke in a pan and starts to "cook" it*)

TEACHER I think S. is cooking artichokes.

S.P. These called artichokes?

TEACHER Yes.

J.G. (*joins S.P. now, goes over to wall where dolls are sitting on beds*) Do you all want supper now? (*B.P. wants to join the play, but this isn't popular with S.P. and J.G.*)

TEACHER J., I think B. would like to play with you.

J.G. (*somewhat resigned*) Sure, there's enough room for everyone.

S.P. I'll make coffee. (*Pouring into pretend cups and using the German word order of his first language*) Here goes coffee in. (*To J.*) You like my coffee?

J.G. Yes.

At this point A.O. joins. She is black. This is the first time I've heard it mentioned or pointed out by the children. J., B., and S. are all feeding white babies. As A.O. comes into the area, S.P. speaks to her.

S.P. And your baby? Your baby is brown. A. is brown.

(*J.G. unconcernedly hands A. the only brown baby*)

A.O. (*whining, sounds near tears*) My baby.

J.G. (*offhandedly*) What's the matter? That's your baby.

S.P. This is my baby. (*slightly sing-song tone of voice as he shows his white baby*)

B.P. I need a white baby.

S.P. (*taunting tone, to A.*) You have a brown one.

J.G. (*sing-song*) We have a white one.

A.O. (*whining*) I want a white one.

J.G. Then we won't give you any dinner!

A.O. (*cradles it, very sad*) My baby . . . .

(*A.O. walks off to the drawing table sadly leaving the brown baby in the housekeeping corner*)

S.P. I'm the mother.

J.G. I need a spoon.

B.P. Give me a fork.

S.P. I'm the mother.

B.P. A knife please, for the baby. (*When he doesn't get immediate results, he says it louder and more insistently*) A knife! (*Finally takes one himself*)

S.P. No, that's my knife!

B.P. (*copies even S.'s tone of voice*) That's my knife!

S.P. I'm . . . my baby wants . . .

B.P. A spoon please, a spoon! (*More and more insistently and louder and louder*) Where the cup go, where the cup go, where the cup go!? (*To himself*) Cup goes over table where the cups go.

(*All three are now "feeding" the "babies," talking to them in such high-pitched, chirpy voices that it's impossible to catch the dialogue*)

J.G. (*returning to normal voice*) Time to go, time to go, time to go to sleep.

S.P. Time to go to sleep.

J.G. Clean up.

S.P. I wanta sleepy.

J.G. (*said over and over as she tucks babies in*) Good night, good night, good night.

Record: Children in Violin Class (December 11, 1975)

The children get their violins from the corner where they are kept and bring them to the center of the room. They find places around the circle and start to open up their cases.

TEACHER (*looking into A.O.'s case*) Where is your rosin?

J.G. (*energetically rosining her bow*) I need fifteen hundred gallons!

S.P. I have no rosin. (*Grinning. He pretends it's lost, then finds it*)

TEACHER Has everybody finished with the rosin?

J.G. (*standing, violin held in "rest position" by her right arm, bow hanging from pointer finger—"bow hook"*) I'm all ready!

TEACHER You beat me, J.!

S.P. (*pretending he can't find violin case*) Mine is all away.

TEACHER Okay, we'll have to start playing without you. We'll miss you, S. (*The teacher gets ready to start the fast movements for getting the violins in position, and S.P., unwatched, gets his instrument ready super fast*)

TEACHER Feet together! Kissing feet, A. That's right. Feet together, everyone. Stop! (*Violins out straight in front of the children*) Turn! (*Violins turned upside-down, ready for next step*) Fly it under your chin! (*The teacher goes around the circle checking each violin for firm grip by chin*) Don't let me get a free violin! (*Trying to gently pull each one away. The violin must be held by the chin so the arms are free to move*)

S.P. I like to do Skier down the Nose today.

This is a game where the teacher checks if the child's head is turned so that he can look down the strings. She traces her finger from the top of the child's head down his nose and, if the violin and head are correctly in line, down the violin strings. If the head is to the right and instrument to the left, the "skier falls off the mountain."

TEACHER S., do you think it would be hard to get a free violin from S.P.?

While S.P. has been talking he has forgotten to hold his violin with his chin. He quickly fixes his position and holds securely with his chin and grins, daring us.

S.P. I fix it!

TEACHER Violins up! Okay, bows in the air! Make a nice slow helicopter right onto the A-string, without a sound. (*Almost whispering*) Remember, not even a tiny sound! Now it's S.'s turn.

The piano introduction to the first variation of *Twinkle, Twinkle Little Star* begins. At the last two beats of the introduction, the teacher says, in rhythm, "Ready, play!" The children play all the way through the first variation on the open A string and do the same thing with all the other variations. The teachers help to guide the bows to stay "on the highway" (a tape is placed under the strings, halfway between the bridge and fingerboard) and "only on the A string."

TEACHER Very nice. Now, freeze! (*The teacher goes around checking violins again for firmness of chin hold*) Would your violin come away, B., if I tried to pull it?

B. quickly adjusts his violin so the teacher can't take it away. But he is too tense about it, so the teacher asks him to flop "like a Raggedy Andy," then resets the violin "in the nest," the right resting spot on each person's left shoulder, so he can hold it more naturally.

TEACHER Let's all be trees swaying in the wind!

She puts her violin gently down on the floor in front of her, and the children follow. They stand in playing position, with feet apart but solidly on the floor while swaying rhythmically "in the wind" and making slow sweeping motions with their arms. While the children continue this the teacher plays *Twinkle* on her violin in time to their movements.

TEACHER Now, let's get on our horses—hold tight to the reins!

She bends her knees and grabs pretend reins in front of her showing how to move to the sixteenth-note rhythm of the fourth variation, then plays it on her violin as the children do the movement. Everyone then sits down in the circle.

TEACHER I'm going to pass a rhythm around the circle. I'll start. Don't let it stop!

The teacher claps the first rhythm of the variations and J.G. takes it up in her turn. B.P. keeps it going very loudly. A.O., not paying close attention, lets the rhythm stop, but after the third try, gets it. A.J. takes it up very exactly, and S.P. finishes it with a grin.

TEACHER Can I see everyone's beautiful bow grips? (*All get their bows, and set their hand positions as best they can*) Remember, camel's hump, wrapped around fingers, and pinky on his head!

These are three keys to a good position. The teacher goes around the circle looking at all the bow hands. J.G. has the best one, so the teacher asks her to help A.O., who seems to like this. A.J. is resistant to help. S.P. has a good grip but needs his fingers better positioned. He lets the teacher help him. B.P. has an extremely tight grip, so the teacher tells him to shake it out, holding his bow for him while he does this. She marks the inside of his fingers with "measle marks" that "you cover with your bow." This intrigues him and he relaxes enough to let the teacher really help him.

J.G. (*having finished helping A.O.*) See, A. has a beautiful bow grip, too!

The teacher stands up with her bow and violin. The children follow.

TEACHER Everyone, bows up in the air—way up high! Now, can you come down without a sound and touch the E string? Now, tip silently—E string to A string (*The teacher is whispering and tipping her bow, and the children follow*) D string, G string, and now way back up to the E string again—without even a tiny sound. (*J.G. and S.P. can do this well, but the others make varying amounts of noise and giggle*) Okay, everyone in rest position and ready to bow, when I say one, two, three! One, two . . . six! One, two . . . zero! One, two . . . three!

Every time the numbers are wrong the children giggle. The anticipation grows until the right combination is announced, when all except A.J. go into a mad scramble to get into rest position as fast as possible. She has had her violin there for a long time, just to be on the safe side. As they all bow, to a slow, even count of "One, two, three," the teacher claps for them.

J.G. Can I play a solo tomorrow?

Record: J.G and B.P. Keeping House (January 8, 1976)

J.G. Here's a tomato. Eat it, eat it! (*Shoves it at B.P., who takes tomato, grins, looks all around, and invents other things to do with it besides eat it. He looks very nervous, has a tight grin on his face*) Eat this tomato!! (*Gets fake-mad, and puts the tomato into the cooking pot from which she had grabbed it. To herself*) Now I'm going to put this back, and not anything for him if he doesn't like my cooking. (*B. comes over, grins, and takes tomato, a chagrined look on his face. J.G. says firmly, in a self-satisfied tone*) Good. You're eating.

B.P. (*whining*) I ate already.

J.G. (*eyes raised and lowered in disgust, mouth tight and determined, pointing to the doll*) You make the little girl eat!

B.P. Okay. (*He feeds doll*) We need some syrup.

J.G. (*screwing up her features in a sneer*) Yuk! Syrup in my food! (*She dumps it out*)

B.P. (*subdued*) You need some fruit. (*Gets fruit from basket, while J.G. delivers cooked food to teacher, to her surprise*)

J.G. (*to teacher, impatiently*) Eat it, it's for you. Eat it, eat it, eat it!

B.P. (*fussing with fruit and vegetables from baskets. Then he gets a "cooked" tomato on a plate and puts knife, fork, and spoon beside it. He gives it to the teacher*) Here.

J.G. (*to herself, back at the stove*) Bunny rabbits eat carrots. (*She comes over to the teacher, now down on her knees and speaking in a squeaky, mouselike voice*) I'm a bunny rabbit, I'm a bunny rabbit.

B.P. (*from the stove*) You want some soup?

J.G. (*sits down to table. B. serves the soup, J. drinks*) Delicious. Thanks. (*She goes to the dress-up-clothes area*) Sorry. You can't come. I'm going to work.

B.P. I'm going to keep the house.

J.G. (*throwing on a man's hat, tie, and gloves*) Okay, take care of the babies for me. (*Going off and up the steps to the fire escape*) Bye, bye . . . BYE! (*B.P. busies himself with cooking while J.G. rides the "bus," the steps serving as seats. Suddenly she jumps up and strides back to the kitchen*) Hi!

B.P. I'm cooking for the babies.

J.G. You know what? It's snowing outside. You want to take the kids out?

B.P. (*looking very worried*) I go with you?

J.G. Of course. Going to make a snowman. Going to put all the babies in snowsuits.

B.P. We have to put warmer clothes on the babies. (*Both put more clothes on the dolls and walk out the door with them*)

Records: Final Summary (January 22, 1976)

J.G. has taken giant steps in development since she came to school in the fall. She has left behind her early hesitation and need for reassurance before proceeding with her own work. She has warm but not clinging relationships with children and adults and is a thoroughly charming person whose very special personality lends joy, humor, and imagination to our school. J. at first needed to show her dissatisfaction with things not being exactly as she wished by pouting, going limp, and hanging her head down, a frown on her face. She doesn't seem to need this trick any longer, or at least she has grown able to hold it in check. She enjoys school, calling it "my school," and uses her lively enthusiasm and inventiveness to make the most of this experience and to share it with the others in the class. She has even learned to laugh at herself—something many an adult cannot do, and something J. could hardly have done a year ago.

She is a natural as a leader *and* a teacher. She is not obnoxious in her leadership, though—she has real charisma. People simply enjoy watching her, and following her is usually fun, too. Using her power in mostly positive ways, she pulls others along with her enthusiasm. She seems to love living the richest, fullest life possible, and that spirit rubs off on anyone around her.

J.G. likes herself too, but is not so self-centered that she can't see beyond her own concerns. Her confidence has grown as she's been able to do more and more tasks well. She piles little successes upon little successes to make big ones. These accomplishments have increased her willingness to persist until she understands something well. The confidence that has come from this has provided an impetus for a longer and longer attention span.

Her self-awareness has grown a great deal this year, too. J. has learned to sit back and enjoy others' efforts without having to share the limelight with them. For a while, in mid-fall, we became worried that she was much too concerned with being first, having the best or the most, and even dominating the character of the class. Other children took up the challenge, however, and asserted themselves more, particularly in Show and Tell, where J.'s presence was all pervasive. Now, except for her treatment of B.P., who is maddeningly persistent in his adoration of her, we feel there is a better balance between her personality and the personalities of the other children in the room. We hope the competition A.J. seems to feel with J.G. will diminish when other children join the class in February. The incident of the brown baby, in which A.O. was so distraught and J.G. didn't attempt to console her, has never been repeated. Before and after this, J.G. played happily with A.O., although she wasn't much interested in her. And S.P. chose the "brown baby" to play with the very next day!

J. began the year easily growing discouraged as she fumbled with scissors and other tools that required small muscle coodination. She found small motor movements difficult but wanted to overcome this when she saw older children and adults doing the things she wanted to do with these tools. Although she is still least patient with academic work, she loves experimenting with the Cuisenaire rods and with writing. She "reads" stories to other children, mostly from memory, but is beginning to notice key words in books and want them written down for her.

J.G. likes adults and uses them as rich resources of information as well as companions with whom she can share a good conversation. J. doesn't suddenly take on a different manner with adults. She is equally natural with everyone, no matter what their age. She gets inspiration, ideas, and language from adults and is very happy when they praise her. Her response to authority has undergone a considerable change since September. Now there seems to exist an unwritten understanding that if we all treat each other reasonably, no authority will have to be imposed. J., of all the children, understands this particularly well.

Generally, J.G. gets along well with other children. There is no denying she is competitive, but I think she has learned to keep this competition under control. She wants to do everything the best she can, but she also wants others to succeed too. At her best, her obvious leadership of the class inspires the other children with its energy and enthusiasm. At her worst, she seems to be running a kind of benevolent dictatorship, her message, "This is for your own good!" She can be a preacher in Show and Tell and a bossy and impatient parent in dramatic play, but she is equally capable of the warmest generosity and compassion. She could use more tolerance for those less strong and expressive than she is. We have begun talking about other people's feelings in the session we call Meeting with the intention of using this neutral setting to discuss conflicts that have come up at other times. Meeting provides children with an opportunity to share thoughts, feelings, and experiences with the entire group.

J. will have to make an adjustment in her view of herself in the classroom before she goes to kindergarten next year. It is doubtful she will be the unquestioned leader next year that she is now. We hope she will not need to be so self-assertive by then. We expect to see considerable changes when new children join the class in February.

J.G. loves hearing and telling stories, doing the latter with great dramatic flair and a highly expressive verbal skill that can take your breath away, it's so inventive. She loves moving to music, singing, playing her violin, art projects, and outdoor play. She has come a long way this year in acquiring academic skills, enjoying lottos, puzzles, Math games, and writing. She has more and more patience for working out intellectual problems on her own, and she sits quietly at a table for longer and longer periods of time. (But she is so gregarious that this is still not easy for her.) J. has largely mastered early problems with holding and manipulating scissors, paint brushes, and pencils. We have approached J.'s need to strengthen her left-hand fingers for violin playing through frequent use of clay and finger-strengthening games.

J.'s greatest love seems to be dramatic play, which she begins in the housekeeping areas and pursues all over the two rooms. Outdoor play time is another rich opportunity for this exciting activity, which is full of interesting ideas and language. Continually recurring themes are family, mother, father, and baby. J. switches roles and moods, but is usually in a position of power. Very occasionally she'll play a helpless little creature with a squeaky voice, and you feel she wants to be cuddled and protected. The intensity of J.G.'s involvement in this playing of roles is so great that the other children seem in awe of her during this activity and afraid to interrupt.

J. is insatiably curious about the world around her. She reasons well and shows that she is quite clear about the basic temporal, spatial, and cause-and-effect concepts. She has an extraordinary memory, as shown by her unusual ability to remember the details of stories in sequence with a high degree of accuracy. Her visual, auditory, and tactile perception are well developed. Everything that touches her senses affects her intensely and is immediately thrown back to the world through her own very unique expression of her feelings. J.'s language can be highly poetic and even epigrammatic at times. It is always extremely inventive.

J.G. seems to be able to step easily from the world of fantasy to reality and back again. She is clear about what is "pretend," and enjoys being a part of both worlds. J. is a vibrant, happy, stable child who has enormous potential for great happiness and success in a rich and exciting life ahead.

Update (May 24, 1976)

The records show J.G. to have been much more in command of the class in the first semester than she is now. We watched her grow from a child who would pout and go limp if she couldn't have her way or didn't want to do something, to an unusually articulate child with strong tendencies toward being a benevolent dictator. By January,though, she had clearly also learned plenty about sharing and concern for others, although she was the unquestioned leader of the group.

Then, in early February, six new and very young (only one had reached three years) children joined the group, and J.'s face fell visibly. The oldest in the class, she went into a pout that lasted almost six weeks, covering her ears when the little ones were too noisy, throwing disgusted looks their way before going to sit in a corner, and generally losing a lot of the vibrant enthusiasm, imagination, and humor she had always brought to the class before the new arrivals "wrecked everything" (her words). She went from a child whose colorful language included phrases like, "I was scared down the shiver!" to the pouting, limp creature of her first days with us.

Gradually, through a real need on the part of the younger children for help in getting adjusted to a new classroom; perhaps through our efforts to make available special, more grown-up activities for the older children alone; and also because J. is too irrepressible to hold down for long, a more realistic balance was achieved. She was no longer Queen of the School, but could go about her business in a more normal way, finally even seeking out younger children (who had adored her from the first) to play with her. It was a tough year for J., but it gave her a series of experiences that will probably prepare her better for kindergarten next year than she would have been had she left us in January when she enjoyed, if cheerfully, such uncontested authority.

AFTERWORD

In writing this book I have thought back over all my experiences in thirteen years of The Suzuki Pre-School. From this rich past, I feel a need to pull together the truths most essential to the foundation of the school. What I have attempted in this book is to stand back from the day-to-day life of an early childhood classroom and generalize about what has been most important there. For me this is very difficult: to try to see the school objectively.

Aside from the great personal rewards anyone working with very young children receives, I feel we have discovered, through our particular school, some principles that can apply much more generally to all kinds of early education, in all kinds of settings.

It has been important to us above all to let children develop at their own pace. We have always observed that they rise to inspiration and stimulation; that nobody seeks mediocrity. Sensitive teachers must be ready to shape the educational experience of each child in partnership with caring parents. The actual learning is done most effectively one step at a time, a building-block approach. Such education gives children the confidence they need for the rest of their lives, and it can make later relearning—costly in human as well as financial terms—quite unnecessary. If high standards are set in the preschool years, a child will have a taste for maintaining such standards from that time on.

These qualities and elements are not unique to The Suzuki Pre-School. Although our school has had a special advantage in combining the Suzuki approach to music with principles of early education as practiced by sensitive teachers anywhere, there is no reason why its successes could not be experienced far beyond its own walls.

America is now facing a crisis in education. In our search for higher standards of education and more effective techniques, we have to start somewhere. I propose, quite simply, that we begin at the beginning—with the earliest education of America's youngest children. If preschool education of real quality becomes a priority in this country, a ripple effect will spread out and up through the higher levels of our educational system. Retraining and remedial teaching of high school or even college students who have never received an adequate educational start comes too late and is rarely more than minimally effective. For students who have begun on the right track in preschool, who have developed good educational habits through step-by-step learning, and who have acquired a sense of confidence in their own abilities, remedial work at a later stage should be unnecessary.

Young children are sensitive, thoughtful human beings who respond beautifully to an equally sensitive and thoughtful environment. They are worth everything to our future as a nation, and they deserve to be given only the best education with the finest teachers we have. Developing an effective support system for the efforts of parents toward rearing their children in the best way they know is an essential first step if we want children to be truly successful in their lives. Parents need a strong government-initiated professional and educational backup for the most challenging job in the world: being the first and most important teachers of this nation's children. And until preschool teachers have the finest training possible and are paid as if earliest education were more important to the country even than college education, we may continue to waste one generation after another. If we Americans were to mobilize behind education, making it as crucial a matter to us as it is to the Japanese, the educational experiences of our children would be the challenging and exciting adventures they ought to be. It's natural for people to respond with eagerness to that kind of energy and success in their lives, and unnatural to be resigned to mediocrity and illiteracy.

In a classroom of two- , three- , and four-year-olds, one sees none of this resignation. Quite the reverse! These children constantly exhibit a natural eagerness, cheer, and industry that they could so easily keep all their lives.

There could be a Suzuki feeling to all educational activity, naturally blending together the diverse parts of children's lives into a unified whole. If all children, with their parents, could receive the Suzuki "habit of action" as a present at birth, many of the problems known as "learning disabilities" would probably never appear, and the need for later remedial work would largely disappear.

We have no time to lose in helping children find the best in themselves. And we can do this by educating them and their parents in this timeless, natural, and highly effective Suzuki way. For, as Alan Pifer reminds us, "If we deny our children's needs, we deny their humanity."

PART TWO

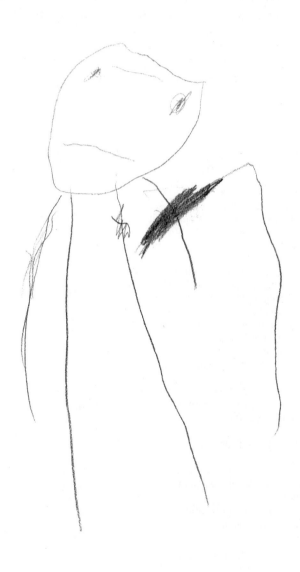

Curriculum Ideas

Some Suzuki Pre-School Special Projects

It is a good idea to have each project filed on an index card—on one side the project name, and on the other, the "recipe," a detailed description of how to go about it. The following list is unfortunately only of project titles. It would not be practical in a book of this limited scope to include all the recipes. There is no substitute for observing these projects as they are done with the children—and for this you are welcome to visit our school.

Art

Potato printing
Plaster in a plastic bag
Cornstarch clay
Straw patterns
Spatter painting
Candle painting
Ghost drawings—white paper, white crayons, black tempera
Paper bag masks
Blot painting
Box sculptures
Print-from-table finger paintings
Basic headband hats, headdresses
Crayon trees, colored paper leaves
Mural to music
Drawing from child model
Portraits of family members
People pictures—life-sized
Outdoor color walk, followed by paintings
Indoor color walk, followed by paintings
Color exhibitions—"Yellow Week," etc.
Color mixing with eyedroppers and food coloring
Colored gel "eyeglasses"
Leaf rubbings
Pipe cleaner sculptures
Play dough
Clay
Collages—found objects, pictures from magazines, etc.
Watercolors
Plaster plaques (handprints)
Weaving—paper strips

Origami
Printing—letters, numbers, shapes, vegetables, fruits, objects in classroom,
    objects from home, etched pieces of styrofoam
Hand and footprints on mural paper
Collage—pre-cut shapes
Torn tissue collages
Cellophane and gel collages
Wax resist paintings with watercolors and Cray-pas
Marbled paper (like rare book endpapers)
Thanksgiving turkeys from handprints
Thanksgiving Indian headdresses from headbands
Christmas and Hanukkah:
    Cards—torn tissue, cellophane/gel
    Christmas trees from green triangles in graduated sizes
    Wrapping Paper—tissue printed with cookie cutters and tempera
    Clay or painted egg-carton candle holders
    Candles from paraffin and red and green crayons
    For the Pre-School tree—construction-paper chains, holiday shapes to
        cut out, clay or play dough cookie cutter decorations, with glitter

Language

Sign-in board
ABC chart with names of children in class
Matching pictures of animals, animal babies
Teacher- and parent-made books
Move objects on table—near, far, under, etc.
Bring something from home that begins with "B," etc.
Chanting days of week, months of year, rhythmically
Puppet theater becoming any kind of store, and labeled as it changes
New rhyme a day or a week
Cookbook with illustrated recipes
Pictures on floor—find all the ones beginning with "P," etc.
Cardboard letter with hook to hang words beginning with that letter
First initial cards—students' names on back
Charts for jobs, birthdays, height, weight, etc.
Chart: "What We Will Do Today"
Pair children whose first initial has same sound
Make a train for days of week, months of year
Start story—let someone else finish
Match animal pictures to appropriate habitat
Teacher-made picture cards to accompany storytelling
Tape record children's stories
Family album for each child
Parents talk about "My Work," with children
Dictated stories about families
Dictionary for each child's favorite words

Book of pictures from home of "favorite things"

Teacher-made worksheets (and workstrips)

Practice with letters—lottos, sandpaper letters on masonite squares, books around letters, etc.

Label objects around the room

Tell story while illustrating it on roll of paper or blackboard

Write parts of letters on blackboard—children finish

Show picture, cover, ask children to describe it

Study one child, send him out of room, try to remember everything about him

Teacher-drawn pictures with a hidden letter

Words for the asking—child adds word to his dictionary

Child tells story of painting—teacher prints in child's words

Teacher-made book around a child's experience

Child retells story just heard

Teacher writes letter on blackboard, helps child trace, child writes alone

Letters drawn in air, sand

Letters painted on mural paper with large house-painting brush (teacher guides first attempts in practice of stroke direction)

Mystery box for letters, words, objects ("What letter does it begin with?")

Child dictates story, teacher prints it on one side of paper—child illustrates on other side

Teacher-prepared book with title: "My Book by . . . "—whenever child requests one

Word and object cards to match

Draw symbol on board. Erase. Child draws from memory

Say several words beginning with same sound—child adds some of his own

"Go Fish" with letters, words (dowel stick with magnet on string, paper clip on letter or word)

Alike, unalike books

Story "reading" by children, from memory

Find the missing part (one part cut off picture)

Draw a form. Change it while children's eyes closed—they must guess what is different

Draw incomplete figure—child completes

Science

Make a musical scale with different amounts of water in same-size glasses

Water play with egg beaters, colander, plastic tubing, sieves, plastic containers, corks, funnels—measuring volume, etc.

Making butter by shaking heavy cream in glass bottle with marble

Experimenting with different states of water (ice melted to water and frozen back to ice, for example)

Something from nature to share with the class

Making pretzels—first play dough, then real pretzel dough

Making our own cookies for a concert—first playdough, then real dough

Making the cooked Pre-School play dough, with the children
Baking gingerbread men at holiday time
Making alum play dough
Making Bank St. College play dough—"add enough oil to make it rubbery"
Making Oriental dumplings, *gyoza,* with help from Japanese mother
Sink and Float game
Measuring—child or part of child (hand, foot, etc.) as unit of measure "How many ways can you measure?"
Lentils on wet cotton—watch the roots grow
Temperature—blindfolded child guesses which water hot, cold, lukewarm
Prisms
Sheets of mirrors
Magnets
Eggs—study before, after boiling
Color experiment—mixing in sink when washing up paint pots
Making pumpkin pie at Halloween or Thanksgiving
Shells—can you hear the ocean?
Protection—turtle shell, egg shell, lobster shell, hard hat, umbrella, etc.
Drop heavy, light objects—how fast do they fall to ground?
Shadows—when are they large or small?
Study of ourselves—what do hands do?, etc.
Radishes planted in potting soil
Grow bean sprouts
Five Senses Exhibit (objects for looking, listening, smelling, tasting, and feeling)
Vibration—tuning fork, larynx, violin string, rubber band, ruler "twanged" off table edge
Pick up something with your toes—pretend you can't use your hands
Pretend you have lost one of your five senses
Blindfolded, guess an object by smell

Math

Book of "1," Book of "2," etc.
Sandpaper numbers on masonite squares
Number Train
Teacher-made geoboard
Cuisenaire Rods chart
"Be" a shape—"Can you stretch wider than you are tall?" (You're a wide rectangle)
Sorting objects for shape, size
"Go Fish" with numerals
Measuring height by legos
Charts for weight, height, sizes of hands, feet, head
Charts for favorite colors, foods, etc.
"Can you find two of something in the room?"
"How many children are in the class today?"

"Let's count to a hundred!" (do it rhythmically)
"I see something that is round," etc.
Bring something round from home, etc.
Same-different games
A few, a lot games
Heavier than, lighter than games
Children imitating action of the math balance
Long-short games, with objects around room
Comparison ("Three Bears," "Three Pigs," etc.)
Objects or children arranged by successive height
Sorting by a chosen characteristic (children as well as objects)
Make shapes with hands in the air
Teacher draws part of a shape, child completes
Teacher describes shape, asks what it is
Attribute Blocks—child describes color, shape, size
Go-together Box (numeral 2, 2 objects, etc.)
Sets —objects that belong in violin case, lunch box, etc. (Pull objects from large Mystery Box)
Things you can do with a collection of five pebbles (arrange in five different ways)
Concentration, or other memory games (with increasing numbers of objects)
Chart with numerals, and cups that hold matching numbers of objects
Shapes—"Tell me what this *isn't.*"
Tangrams
Scale—beans, rice for weights
Teacher-made counting ropes, with 1, 2, 3, etc. knots to count ("Close your eyes and guess how many")
Measuring ribbons—"See if you can find three things that are as long as your ribbon"
Concepts of full, empty
Opposites—big, little; thick, thin—etc.
Large, small—charts of objects in the room
Envelope of shapes cut by each child
Relationshapes—tracing
Unifix Cubes—how tall can you build a tower (how many cubes tall?)
Teacher-made worksheets, task cards on number, work strips
Cuisenaire Rods—worksheets
Child-drawn pictures of Rod constructions
Numerals painted large on mural paper, for practice in direction of strokes
Piaget-type experiments in Conservation—Water Table

Theater Games

Teacher starts a motion, child continues or completes it
Walk and talk as if old, happy, sad, etc.
Role-play various jobs (include being teachers, parents)

One word command cards (child acts out command)
"One part of your body is stuck to the floor . . . "
A picture tells a story—group discussion and movement
Take a ride on a camel, horse, subway, bus, canoe, spaceship, bubble, witches' broom, rainbow, etc.
Look at two, three, or four objects—look away and tell what you saw
Blindfolded, walk through textures of various kinds—what do you feel?
Follow the Leader
Mimed reaction to words: bird, moth, snow, rain, sun, flowers, city, country, beach, violin, mother, father, sister, brother, dog, cat, teacher, etc.
What is the person next to you wearing? (eyes shut)
Role-play getting out of bed, dressing for school, eating breakfast, going to school, etc.
Find the group (one child blindfolded)
Pretend our hands are glued to each other, then move to music
Pretend you are—smoke moving, puppets, shivering, on a trapeze, etc.
Be a melting candle
Wake up parts of your body, starting with your toes
Take a trip up a mountain, through sand, across a brook, getting stuck in mud, to a zoo, etc.
Be a balloon, then pop it with a pin
Be a balloon, then let the air out really slowly
With eyes closed, guess the object put in your hand
"I am going to California and taking . . ." (list and act out objects)
Be a melting icicle
Be a growing plant
Be different things in the wind (a leaf, a snowflake, a heavy immovable object, something bendable, etc.)
Be an animal from "Carnival of the Animals"
Walk like a crooked man, robot, Raggedy Ann or Andy, etc.
Run like a mouse, elephant, etc.
Jump like popcorn, a kangaroo, etc.
Hop like someone with a sore leg
Leap like a deer or over a river
Gallop like a farm horse, circus pony, King's horse, etc.
You are an instrument in the orchestra
How does this music make you feel?
"A wolf just came out of the woods. What would you do?"
"I am a magician, and you are all . . ."
Teacher does an action, child mirrors it
Throw an imaginary object (heavy, light, large, or small)

Large Muscle Coordination

Walk the line (string or rope)—with and without carried objects
Close eyes, point to familiar objects in room
Balance: jump on right then left foot (repeat with eyes closed)

Indian Chief (one child goes out of room, another child becomes leader and group follows clapped rhythms, first child comes back in room and has to guess who is leader. Object: to change rhythms so subtly that leader can't be guessed)

Child stands at blackboard with chalk in each hand, held at eye level. Using both hands simultaneously draw circular motions rotating clockwise and counterclockwise. Draw horizontal lines, going in and out from the center of the body.

Draw to music, fast and slow—watch the drawings change!

Pegs and pegboard—children place pegs in top row, bottom, at corners, on right side, left side, in middle.

Sewing in burlap

Pick up small objects with clothespins (pre-Chopsticks)

Lay pieces of clothes line in a loopy pattern on floor and ask children to step in the loops without touching rope

Children push bean bag across floor first with both feet. Push with right foot, then left foot, then alternating feet. Try to kick bean bag into a circle.

Dribble a ball around markers

Children sit in circle—keep ball in circle by kicking it with their feet (children lean back on hands with feet straight ahead)

Say and point, in rhythm: "I see with my—, I smell with my—, I blink my—, I clap my—," etc.

Fine Muscle Coordination

Weaving with cardboard strips

Sewing cards—commercial and teacher-made

Pick up small objects with eyes closed

Pick-up sticks

Alphabet-noodle collage

Use of chopsticks to pick up various objects around room

Painting with small paint brushes

Dots on finger tips—"tall man" and thumb, etc. (for "eye-glasses" violin game)

Sorting small objects (beads, raisins, etc.) into egg carton sections

Eyedroppers: color mixing

Watercolors on small paper

Origami

Workstrips for practice cutting different patterns with scissors

Striped wallpaper from wallpaper books, for cutting practice

Finger plays (with and without music)

String figures

Finger puppets

Crumple paper with one hand (combine with collage art project)

Pick up small objects—pennies, marbles, beans, etc. Place these in the mouth of a small bottle or through a small opening in a box

Pick up small objects with toes
All the many games used in Violin Class to develop left-hand fingers, particularly finger bouncing, one finger at a time, first on violin shoulder, then on string

Perception

"Who is it?" (guess by voice alone)
Show picture, hide. Can children remember all details?
Five Senses Exhibit
"Can you remember (about family members) color of hair, eyes?," etc.
Bring something from home—soft, hard, round, square, etc.
Walk (or march) around shapes drawn on floor
Study a person carefully—when they leave, can you remember every detail?
Geometric shapes in graduated sizes
Boxes within boxes, dolls within dolls
Scent bottles (two each)—match
Sound cylinders (two each)—match
Matching color swatches (two each)
Arrange objects from heavy to light, with eyes closed
Silence game: "How many sounds can you hear?"
Buttons—sort by color, size, shape, feel
Texture board—match the swatches to the materials on the board
Eyes shut, discriminate teacher-made sounds (keys jangling, chair moving, pencil writing, book closing, paper being crumpled, etc.)
Eyes shut, clap rhythms after teacher (or stamp feet in rhythm)
Cut paper strips 1/2-inch wide. Ask children to paste strips on another piece of paper in shape of a triangle, square, etc.
"Can you see what I see?" "I see something . . . " (round, square, etc.)
"Can you guess what I see?" "I see something . . . " (round, square, etc.)
Children make geometric shapes out of building blocks
Teacher-made puzzles
Mystery Box, with shapes from classroom

Rainy-day Games

Musical Chairs
Simon Says
Indian Chief
Pass the hat to music
Keep rhythm going around circle (clapping, clapping to record, or to teacher's piano or violin or other instrument)
Child blindfolded, rotated. Must say who facing, in circle, when music stops
Ball back and forth across circle—when music stops, out if holding ball
Teacher starts song, points to someone to join in until all singing (then do same thing with subtraction, until nobody singing—silence)
Mime activities in classroom. See if children can guess what you are doing

Teacher starts a song—points to a child to continue or complete

Singing directions (one thing to do) to next person around circle (try to keep in rhythm)

Red Light

Child, blindfolded, marches around inside of circle—where he stops (music stops), that person is "it"

"I am going to California and taking . . . " (each child has to remember all former objects, listing his own at the end of the catalogue

"How did you get there from here?"

"I am a magician and you are all . . . "

Close eyes—point to familiar objects in room

Memory: "How many can you remember?" (Cards with pictures on one side, blank on the other. Teachers can make this game to suit their own individual classrooms)

Find the missing part—one part of picture has been cut off—identify it and teacher shows missing piece

Musical relays with bean bags—use Suzuki recording

Charlie Over the Water

Duck, Goose

General Music

Children teach songs to teachers, other children—"What's your favorite song?"

Finding rhythm in surprising places (outdoor walks, field trips, etc.)

Recording sounds from world outside school—"Can you guess what this is?"

Learning new songs: children hum, while teacher sings

Solo singing (beautiful tone, as with violin)

Catalogue songs and story songs (for example, *One Wide River to Cross*)

Teacher-made songs

Teacher-with-children compositions

Make "finger piano" using tongue depressors of different lengths

Flash cards with pictures of different instruments

Children be instruments—first just sound, then pretend play

Marching Band—children be instruments

Program Music (*Peter and the Wolf, Danse Macabre, Noye's Fludde,* etc.) (first just listen, then move to it)

Dancing to ballet music (two rules: "Ballet dancers don't bump!" and "Freeze when the music stops!")

Rhythms tapped on nose, under chin, on tummy, etc. (Add new place each time through, then do backwards)

Piano plays chords at different tempi—children follow music

Songs: *London Bridge, Here We Go Round the Mulberry Bush, Brother, Come and Dance with Me, Skip to My Lou, Near and Far, Momotaro, Oki na Taiko, One is a Number,* (or say "Finger")

Art work to music

WORKSHEETS

Primary Colors

Find the red dot and draw a circle around it
Color the two yellow bananas
Find the blue triangle and draw a circle around it
Cut out the three blue circles with your scissors
Color the triangle yellow, the square blue and the circle red

Shapes: Circle, Square, Triangle, Rectangle

Cut out the circle with your scissors.
Can you trace this circle? (Shows a circle drawn with dots)
Draw something that is shaped like a circle
Draw a circle and color it red
Put a circle around the red triangle

Names

Name-writing practice—on specially lined paper, dotted line to show
    lower case position
Can you find your name? Draw a circle around it. Names on a sheet (in-
    cludes everyone in class)
How many times can you trace your name?—dotted line name repeated
    several times
Can you find your name hidden in this picture?

Numbers

Put a circle around the 2
Put a circle around the two
Two 2—with a large dotted 2 to trace
When you see two 2 dots together, draw a circle around them
Draw two 2 of something

Letters

Put a circle around the C, using only letters of children's first names
How many times can you trace the C? Dotted line letter repeated several
    times
Put a circle around the C—whole alphabet—capitals
Put a circle around the C—whole alphabet—lower case
Cut out the C with your scissors—drawn very large

SIMPLE EQUIPMENT MADE BY TEACHERS

Mechanical board—for lacing, tying, buckling, zipping
Sound cylinders—plastic medicine bottles covered with contact paper with
    rice, pennies, etc. inside

Texture board—bits of soft, rough, silky, and bumpy materials mounted on a large board

"Cook Book"—with many pictures of delicious foods inside

Color gel see-through boxes—a yellow on top of a red makes an orange, etc.

Bean Bags

Weaving game—board with brads and a leather thong for weaving

Shoe bag cubbies

Sewing cards

Sandpaper on masonite blocks—numbers and letters

Color wheel

Lottos—color, number, shape, sequence, name, matching, letter, etc.

Mystery box

Teacher-made books—color, number, shape, texture, and other subjects of interest (music, dance, children, etc.)

Name chart

How Do They Feel? Pictures that tell a story

How Many Are There? Pictures with a clear number of objects in them

Geoboards

Number cards—1 through 20

Cards with dots—1 through 20

Puppets and painted backdrops for *Hansel and Gretel* and *The Enormous Turnip*

Story cards to illustrate story telling—three or four scenes from the story on large cards

Suzuki Violin Games

This is a partial list of games culled from observation of many fine Suzuki teachers to meet our own need to tailor Suzuki ideas to the special demands of including the violin in a total preschool curriculum. We would not know how to begin crediting the exact person with the exact idea. We hope we can share what has worked for us with the very clear understanding that the same things may very well not work for another teacher. As we have taken what we needed and discarded what wasn't natural to us, we hope others will do the same. In the dozen years of this experimental preschool, we have been constantly evolving new approaches, and we hope to continue to grow in this same way by taking inspiration from new sources around us, and from our own successes and failures.

We've really only just begun, and hope we will never stop changing in favor of what works best for the children.

Posture—Balance

1. Trace child's feet on manila folder in "playing position" to set that position correctly from the beginning. Use the "feet" as position markers until child comes automatically to stand with feet about a foot apart and left foot slightly forward. Have the children leave the "feet" to march around the room following the teacher who is playing *Twinkle*. When the music stops children are told to "Find your feet!"

2. Use the idea "Your head is a balloon!"—child reaches up "to the ceiling, on tiptoe," then slowly brings his feet down flat on the floor without "letting the air out of the balloon." He has pulled himself up to the tallest and straightest possible posture and kept it as he comes down off his toes onto his full feet. The teacher can set a perfect violin position for him now.

3. While the teacher plays, the children go up on tiptoes and down again, to the rhythm of her playing. Later, the teacher pretends that "strings" to all the balloons are attached to the scroll of her violin. Keeping as straight and tall as possible herself, she can get the children to sway in rhythm with her and mirror her posture as she plays.

4. Once the violin is in position under the chin, the teacher takes her

finger and "skis" from the top of the child's head down his nose and down the violin strings. If the skier falls off, the position is not correct. In correct position, the child's nose should point toward the scroll of his violin, which is directly over his left foot; his eyes should look down the strings of the violin. The teacher can say, "Don't let the skier fall off the mountain this time!"

5. The teacher may say, "Button the button into your neck" to give the idea of the violin being as natural a part of the body as another arm. "No air space" should be between the violin and the child's neck, as his chin holds the instrument securely in place. (The "button" is the end pin that is attached by a piece of gut to the tailpiece, which in turn holds the tightened strings in the necessary tension.)

6. The teacher says: "Hands on head," "Hands on shoulders," "Hands on waist," etc., giving fast commands.

7. The teacher "makes a necktie" with her violin, letting it droop down more or less in front of her rather than covering her left shoulder with the instrument and bringing her chin to it as she should. A child is asked to fix the teacher's bad position—usually being very strict with the teacher, and often learning more this way than through being directed and guided in his own positioning of the violin.

8. Hold "no hands" to the count of five; later extend to the count of ten, then twenty-five.

9. Use a mirror and have the child put the "head" (scroll of his violin) straight up to the glass and see "someone else just like you." If posture droops, the child fixes that "other person in the mirror."

10. One child gets into his best violin position, then freezes. Another child then checks his position and helps correct it wherever necessary. Then the two children switch roles. In helping others, the child's own posture is likely to improve.

11. The teacher puts an imaginary object on each child's head to balance as he walks "as tall as you can so you won't drop it." The child walks around the circle in this fashion. Real bean bags can be placed on the child's head, too.

12. Each child walks across the balance beam, arms out to his sides. The teacher then plays a game in which there is a pretend beam and the children have to try to keep the same feeling. A rocking platform can also be used for balance.

13. As the teacher plays *Twinkle, Twinkle, Little Star,* the children "get

onto their playing feet!" and sway to the music. Sometimes this is done with their mothers standing directly in front of them, holding both hands and swaying with them. Later, a modified form of this motion adds freedom to violin playing. Feet are spread just far enough apart and the left foot is slightly forward, to give a feeling of perfectly comfortable balance so that some rhythmic movement can be part of the playing and one is not rooted stiffly to the ground.

14. The teacher teaches the children to follow her position with their eyes as they play. She always stands to the children's left, with the head of her violin toward them, so that they don't sacrifice their good position to watch her.

15. The teacher plays a game of "Reach to the ceiling! Curl up on the floor! Reach to the ceiling again!" This exercise is designed to limber up the body and make heads alert.

16. The children stand on one foot to the count of five, then on the other. Later they do this with the violin in no-hands position (held entirely by the chin), and still later while they play a piece.

17. When helping a child through the steps used in getting the violin up onto his shoulder, the teacher is usually directly in front of the child until he is ready to turn his head left and put his chin down on the chinrest. Then the teacher moves to his left so that he can continue to look straight at her and keep his good position.

18. The teacher puts a book where the violin should be, covering the left shoulder, as child marches to music without dropping it and keeping it up straight.

19. Pretending to be holding real violins in rest position, the children go through the four steps to playing position and "pretend play" while the teacher actually plays. Unencumbered by the actual instrument, they can watch the teacher and move freely following her motions, usually quite accurately.

20. The teacher introduces the bow through child-size cups and pours pretend juice—"What's your favorite flavor?"—into each cup. Usually one child wants to "spill the juice" right at the beginning, but most go along with three or four exercises to be used in the future with real bows—Elevators (straight up and down in front of the child, slowly), Rockets to the Moon (still straight up and down, but faster, and ending up without warning on top of the head—straight "like an antenna"), Stirring the Pudding (a circular action with the cup still straight—out, around, and back in toward the body again). Then comes the time to "spill a little juice" (tip the cup just a little and quickly

return to the up-and-down position again). These are all preparations for a free-moving bow arm—the sort that will produce big, beautiful tone.

21. The children pass a violin around the circle, each one getting it into a perfect no-hands position before he can pass it on. When the music stops, the person holding the violin is out.

Tone

1. The teacher plays her open E string and sings the tone. Then she plucks it near the ear of each child making it "ring like a bell," and the child sings the tone.

2. Pizzicato is taught very early. The child holds the violin in his lap and plucks the E string or A string. Then D and G strings are added. We usually introduce the string tones without violins first: "The elevator goes from the roof to the basement" (hand held up high is E string, "the roof"; down a bit is A string, "second floor"; down further is D string or "first floor"; finally, hand held low is G string or "the basement"). Each step down is sung by everyone as the teacher plucks the sound on her own violin. On the violin, the children put right thumbs upside down on the side of the finger boards and use the pointer finger to pluck and sing: "E string, A string, D string, G string," and back up to E again. A lot of emphasis is put on beautiful sound right from the beginning—the connection between a "wiggling" tuning fork and vibrating string seems to be easy to show, and the children enjoy becoming a tuning fork themselves, arms straight up in the air, wiggling back and forth together.

3. The teacher asks the child, "Can you make it ring?" right from the first time he pulls the bow across an open string.

4. The teacher says something like, "Don't squeeze the strawberry!" when the child first holds the bow and tries to grab it. By continually trying to soften and shape the child's bow grip the teacher is setting the child's hand into the natural balanced control over the bow which produces good tone.

5. The teacher plays a harmony accompaniment to whatever the child is playing, right from the beginning. Children appreciate the enhanced, more beautiful sound, and want to play longer.

6. The teacher suddenly plays bad, scratchy tone in the middle of playing *Twinkle* the best she can. The children have to tell her why it sounds so terrible ("Yukky" is the word, even with two- and three-year olds). She asks the child to show her how to do it better.

7. To get the feeling of "heavy bow," the child turns his bow around, the frog in the air, and plays this way. He later tries to keep the same feeling with the bow held in the correct way.

8. When there is a scratchy, pushed tone, the teacher says something like, "Your violin is hurting."

9. When the child gets a little more advanced, he can pluck an open string—"Make it ring like a bell"—then play the same tone with his bow—"Make it really sing"—and then pluck again to see if he still has that ringing, big sound.

10. To get big tone, one needs a free-moving bow arm. The teacher says, "Put some oil in your elbow!" and pretends to do just that in the inside of the elbow. The child has already done exercises without the violin—"Pat your tummy"—with one arm moving freely out and back in, out and in, over and over. The teacher may move the child's lower arm to see if it has "enough oil in it now" and helps him move the bow on the strings so that he can pull, not push, the sound out and get a big, clear tone.

11. Each movement of the bow is prepared so that the tone will be good. An exercise called Helicopters has the child holding the bow horizontally over the violin and moving it straight up and down over the instrument. When he is ready to play, he brings the bow down on the string "without a sound," stopping it before moving it on the string. Later, he practices tipping the bow without a sound from string to string to get good, clear string crossing and to avoid spoiling good tone with extraneous sounds.

12. The teachers occasionally improvise on their own violins for the children, or play a duet with one of the first Suzuki pieces. One day they played a duet on two of the children's small violins, which at first delighted all the children. Then the two whose violins were being used looked extremely unhappy and one said, "You shouldn't use my violin like that," so we haven't repeated this game.

13. To get the correct bow grip, the teacher generally uses two ideas the children know: "Make a Snoopy dog with your bow hand" and "the camel story." For Snoopy, the middle right hand fingers curve over the thumb, the pointer and pinky up in the air as "ears." When the child has this position, the teacher can slip the bow into his hand and put "pinky on his head" and "pointer wrapped around." The curve of the thumb is already there. The camel story has the child turn his hand and bow over and move the stick along his hand until the frog of the bow comes right under his thumb, bent like "a camel's hump." The thumb goes down on "the silver fountain" where "the camel is

drinking—he is so thirsty!" The bow is turned over and rested, hair on child's left shoulder. All the other fingers are wrapped around the stick except the "pinky on his head." The teacher pushes a slight space between "pointer and tall man" to complete a perfect bow grip—absolutely essential for a big, beautiful, balanced tone.

14. The teacher plays the Match My Tone game with the children. "Make it just like mine" or "Make it better than mine," which is more fun.

Intonation

1. The teacher takes her tuning fork and taps it on her knee. Then she rests it on her violin bridge to amplify the tone for the whole class. This is something the children immediately want to do themselves. The children all sing the A of the tuning fork as the teacher puts it on each violin bridge. The coordination of turning the vibrating fork over without touching the prongs and thus stopping the sound is very difficult, but children will usually struggle to try to master it. They never seem to grow tired of the tuning fork.

2. The teacher plays one of the first two open strings learned and asks the children to guess which one she is playing—first with eyes open, then with eyes shut. Finally, she plays the tone behind their backs. Later, the children can guess what finger she is playing if they are given the sound of the open string first. A few children can even guess accurately without that hint.

3. The children sing a scale (usually D Major, since A is too high), D-one-two-three-A-one-two-three-three-two-one-A-three-two-one-D, as the teacher plays and sings it. Or the teacher may sing and move her hand from floor to "as high as you can reach," and back down "the steps" to the floor again. Both tone (the emphasis is on a light, clear tone) and intonation are practiced in this way.

4. The tuning fork is as important for intonation as for developing a good tone—as are singing and plucking open strings and "being" a scale. Teacher-played harmony parts to whatever the child is playing help him hear what sounds are exactly in tune.

5. After singing the sounds of the open strings day after day, the children can recognize when the violin needs tuning.

6. Not long after the beginning of lessons, the teacher can tune her violin with her bow holding the tone as she moves the pegs into perfect tune, and stop when the children tell her it sounds right. She may show them how the tone sounds all dead if the strings are not in tune—and how the tone rings when they are in tune.

7. Singing is done continually, in and out of the violin class—the more the better, it seems, for implanting a firm idea of correct intonation. Children sing words to songs they will be playing later on the violin. As they learn fingering they sing finger numbers to the notes of *Twinkle*.

8. The children love to correct the teacher's bad intonation—the teacher lets a child push her too low or too high finger into the right position for the correct tone, the teacher bowing the string all the while so the child can hear when the correct pitch is reached.

Listening-Observation

1. Without a sound, the teacher takes her violin from rest position and takes it through the steps to playing position—the children have to follow with their eyes, to know what to do.

2. The teacher stands behind a child's back, clapping or playing a rhythm which the child immediately copies.

3. The teacher purposely jumbles the directions for getting the violin into playing position, to see if the children are still able to follow her. Instead of "Stop! Turn! Fly it in! Chin!" it may be "Stop! Rest Position! Stop! Turn! Rest Position!" etc.

4. As soon as the children can play the first rhythm on open E string (where the bow arm is in the most restful position, thus the first string to be learned), the teacher will see if they can go through a beginning-to-play routine that will continue in all of their group lessons to come. First she plays one repetition of a rhythm. Then she says, "Ready and play" (in rhythm) and the children follow her, playing exactly one rhythm, and taking their bows straight off the string immediately afterward. This is also a preparation for any performing the children will do, in workshops and concerts, where the teacher will lead them in the same way. Eventually, they will be able to play together without a leader doing anything but getting them started—they will have learned so much about listening to each other.

5. The teacher plays the One-two-three! game in many forms. The first and most obvious is using it to get the children from a sitting to a standing position in a group. One-two-anything else but three means don't move, so the teacher gives lots of wrong combinations before finally arriving at the right one. The children's attention seems to increase with the anticipation.

6. "Stop playing when the music stops!"—you really have to be listening hard or you'll be left playing alone.

7. The teacher starts one piece and suddenly switches into another or in some way changes it—can the children tell?

8. With the bow held vertically in the air, the teacher "plays" a rhythm and sees if the children can guess which one it is.

9. A child in the middle of the circle holds his violin with his chin alone ("no hands"), while the others march around him. When the music stops, the child in the middle quickly switches places with the one in front of him.

10. "Where is the . . . ?" game done with violin or bow. In a chanting voice and in rhythm, the teacher says, "Where is the bridge?" and the children answer while pointing to that spot on the instrument, "Here is the bridge!" etc. The last part of the bow or violin to be mentioned is always the part you can't touch: "Where is the hair?" The children love to say, "Don't touch the hair!" over and over again, while they move their hands over the top of the hair—almost touching but not quite.

11. When a child is ready to learn fingering, tapes are put on the violin fingerboard to show the exact location of pitches in the key of A-Major, which will carry him through his first nine pieces. His left hand position is set, with "fingers on their heads," and faces are drawn on each fingernail, corresponding in color to the tape underneath. Although he must rely primarily on his ear for finding the correct pitch, this color coding helps his eye locate the right spot as well.

12. A tape "highway" is put on the violin under the strings midway between bridge and fingerboard, to show "where the bow travels." Another tape is put on the bow at the middle—at the point of the square of that child's arm in relation to his violin when held in playing position. The child must see that the bow stays "on the highway."

13. The teacher starts a rhythm and passes it around the circle—each child clapping it once. As this is practiced, the children can do it without losing the beat.

14. Follow the leader: The teacher leads a march around the room, the children following her wherever she goes and whatever she does. She may have the children clapping a steady rhythm the whole time or keeping a basic beat with their feet, while turning, squatting, standing on one foot and then the other, or switching direction.

15. The teacher sees if children can answer questions while continuing to play a rhythm on an open string, or while holding the violin no hands. Later, children can play fairly complex pieces while doing the

same thing and not lose the beat. An astonishing result of this kind of training was shown at a concert of Suzuki violinists from Japan—they were divided into two groups to play the Bach Double Violin Concerto. As they played their teacher clapped his hands at random to signal switching of parts, Violin I and Violin II. This they did without a single break in the music!

16. The distinction between loud and soft can be made by standing up to play the loud and sitting for the soft. By clapping rhythms "so softly I almost can't hear you," the children seem to hear them better.

17. The children put thumb and another finger together "on their heads" to make a circle which they can look through—"eye-glasses." They then bounce the two fingers together very close to their ears. They have to be very quiet to hear the "tap-tap" sound.

18. A whole lesson had to be led in a whisper one day because the teacher had laryngitis. The children were working so much harder than usual not to miss a thing, that the teacher now uses this method occasionally even if she's feeling fine.

19. A child fixing the teacher's bad position is much stricter than the teacher herself would ever think of being. The child notices anything that is even slightly wrong.

20. A child will work harder on his position if another child is watching to see if he has everything right. They then switch roles so there is no feeling that some children are better than others.

Fine Muscle Coordination

1. Spiders and Chickens Scratching are games to get all the fingers moving quickly, even before the violin is played. The teacher leads *Eensy Weensy Spider* with the appropriate finger play, aiming for fast-moving independent fingers. Chickens Scratching is done with fingers on the floor where children can see their fingers' separate movements better.

2. "One thumb, one finger, one hand" is a song that involves finger play in such a rhythmic way the children work very hard to keep hand motions up to the tempo of the music.

3. The teacher says, "Thumbs up! Ones up! Twos up! Threes up! Fours up!" as fast as she can, and the children have to stick up the correct finger as she does. Speed is increased as the children become more used to the game.

4. Left hand finger bouncing—first thumb and one, thumb and two, etc. Later fingers bounce "on their heads" on the violin shoulder when

the violin is being held in playing position, and finally directly on the strings when fingering is begun. All serve to strengthen the fingers for the "throw down, spring back motion" from the knuckles of the hand that allows the player to hold down the string securely without sacrificing a relaxed hand and wrist.

5. Making a Snoopy Dog with the fingers of the right hand, to approximate the correct bow grip, is very hard for the children at first. After several repetitions, they begin to be able to cover their thumbs with their middle fingers. Finally Snoopy can go "bite, bite, bite the bow!"—middle fingers and thumb opening and shutting, while pointer and pinky serve as ears.

6. The teacher puts marker dots on the inside of the child's right hand— he can "cover the marks" with his bow and get the right bow grip.

7. The child guides his bow up and down through a circle made by the teacher's two hands to see if he can keep it straight without touching her hands. This vertical up-and-down motion of the bow learned first as Elevators is speeded up to become Rockets and is basic to all bowing.

8. To be sure the child's little finger is properly curved on his bow, he does "pinky push-ups" on the bow, pinky "on his head." This exercise can be done most easily while the bow is resting on the child's left shoulder, where he can watch the motion of his fingers very closely.

9. Pizzicato requires a great deal of fine muscle coordination. The pointer finger of the right hand runs along the string and then under it, lifting it and letting go in a circular motion to get a ringing, clear tone. The children first pluck one string at a time, when asked to find it. They later sing, "E string, A string, D string, G string," while plucking those open strings. As soon as a child can use fingers, new pieces are learned first with pizzicato. Later, the left-hand pinky is used to pluck the G string "like a clock striking twelve!" and thereby much strengthening it.

Quick Response

1. Simon Says gets very fast reactions but takes a long time for very young children to learn. They don't really see why they can't follow the teacher's movements just because "Simon didn't say so." The teacher usually substitutes another game which simply leaves out the Simon Says complication. The children follow her very quick changes of movement as fast as they can—"Hands on heads! Hands on your shoulders! Hands on your knees!" etc.

2. "Stand up when you hear one-two-three!"

3. "One-two-three!" The right arm sweeps in a large curve from the child's side up to the top of his head, and back down again. This is also good for freeing the bow arm and general loosening up of the body.

4. March—switch rhythms or directions without losing the beat.

5. The children's violins and bows are on the floor in front of them. At the signal "One-two-three!" they have to get them into rest position as fast as they can. (The first signals were probably something like "One-two-seven!" or "One-two-zero!" increasing the suspense.) Later the same game is used for getting violins quickly into playing position.

6. The steps used for getting the violin into playing position are done very quickly. Finally the child can put his violin directly on his left shoulder and turn his head to it. In performances children can be ready to play very fast as a result of all this practice in quick response.

7. After the violin is securely in playing position and the child wants to use his left-hand fingers, he first rests his left hand on the violin "shoulder," fingers "on their heads." He prepares his fingers for the fingering movements they will be doing by bouncing them on the shoulder, pretending the violin is "hot—don't get your fingers burned!" This gives him the "throw down" and quick "spring back" motion he will need for fingering.

8. When fingers are ready, the signal "Whoosh!" tells the child to slide them very quickly down the fingerboard to the position of the tapes. By making this move so quickly, the child can preserve the correct position of the fingers as it was set up on the violin shoulder. The left hand should be entirely relaxed, violin still held only by the chin.

9. When fingering is first taught, "bow, fingers, same string" and "finger first, then bow," are the rules. The child can take as long as he needs to prepare the finger, but it must be securely down on the right tape and the bow on the correct string, before it moves. Then it moves up-to-tempo!

10. The teacher calls the bow a train and the fingers people who want to get on and off the train. This very much helps the child to understand that the finger must be set and the bow stopped on the string before the note can be played. To aid this learning, the scale, the first music played with fingers, is first played with a stop between each note, giving the child ample time to prepare the next note, but the actual playing is done up-to-tempo so the music never lags.

11. The teacher moves around the circle clapping one rhythm with each child, then moves from child to child randomly, to see if the children are still wide awake and can do this without missing a beat.

12. The teacher pretends she doesn't know which fingers to use for *Twinkle,* and the child has to put the teacher's fingers down correctly, one at a time, before she can move her bow. The child sees how quick the response of the finger needs to be, since the teacher is keeping this game in rhythm so it won't bog down.

13. The teacher plays a rhythm behind a child's back—he has to play it back to her immediately.

14. The teacher and the children play one repetition of a rhythm, then immediately raise the bow off the string. Then the bow is reset on the string, but does not move until the next signal is given ("Ready and Play," said in rhythm).

Rhythm

1. The children sit Indian-style, and first clap rhythms on their knees, which is easier than clapping hands together. Words are used that fit the rhythm. For the first variation of *Twinkle,* for example, we often use, "I like choc-'late ice cream."

2. Some other words that we use to fit the rhythms are: (second variation) "My name is Janie, and my name is Douglas . . . "; (third variation) "Run, Jimmy, Run, Jimmy"; (variation four) "Watermelon, watermelon." These are most commonly in use, but it is a good idea to make up new words to the rhythms all the time, for freshness and to be sure one set of words doesn't become rigidly accepted as the only possible one to use.

3. Rhythms can be tapped on head, shoulders, on the floor with a dowel stick—any place.

4. From the very beginning the teacher establishes a basic beat. "Get on your marching feet" she says, and first the children march in place. When they have the beat securely established, they march around the room following the teacher, who is very likely playing the first variation of *Twinkle* on her violin and keeping the basic beat with her feet. Later the children can clap the rhythm with their hands while keeping the beat with their feet. Still later they march while playing their violins, the beat kept going by their feet.

5. Rhythms can be played in the air with a pretend bow or a dowel stick, or even with a real bow. Later, the child can play whole phrases of a piece in the air.

6. Rhythms can be played with thumb and one finger bouncing on "their heads." Following this, the teacher often does the same rhythm with thumb and one, thumb and two, etc.

7. The *Twinkle, Twinkle Little Star* theme is played by the teacher while children sway back and forth to it, standing on their "playing feet" (manila folders, at first).

8. The Watermelon rhythm is played. The teacher says, "Get on your horse and hold on tight to the reins!" and the children's knees bend in time to the rhythm of the sixteenth notes.

9. When the children are a little more advanced, it is possible to divide the class in half—one group clapping the basic beat while the other claps the rhythm of the piece.

10. The whole class claps following the teacher and changes rhythms with her. This is a prelude to Indian Chief—a game where one child goes out of the room while another starts the group clapping, changing rhythms when he does. The child outside returns and has to guess who is the leader.

11. "Play the drum with your feet!" is a game the children can't do right away. It requires that their feet, not hands, do the rhythms.

12. While first learning to rosin the bow, the child can rosin it in rhythm, while the teacher plays.

13. The teacher stands behind the child's back and plays a new rhythm he's never heard. The child usually can copy it quite easily and make up his own new rhythms too.

14. Children do finger bouncing on the shoulder of the violin when the violin is in playing position, bouncing fingers to all the rhythms of the variations. After they can bounce all of the fingers, they bounce one at a time, which is much harder.

15. Although the Suzuki record goes at a very fast tempo, and children are advised not to try to play along with it, that speed is fine for marching or clapping.

16. Rhythms may be played first moving the bow on the child's left shoulder, so he can watch his elbow opening and closing as he plays, a movement so important for big, free tone.

Large Muscle Coordination

1. Before playing, the children usually do loosening up calisthenics to make the body totally relaxed, posture tall, and mind alert for playing. A typical series of these exercises might be: standing up on tiptoes to "reach the ceiling" and then flopping the upper part of the body loosely down from the waist, arms swinging back and forth completely relaxed, then quickly back up on your toes again. "Flying like a bird," arms making wide circles in the air, and a fast game of Simon Says are other good quickeners and relaxers.

2. The steps used to get the violin into playing position, "Stop! Turn! Fly it in! Chin!" require a lot of coordination. "Fly it in" means aiming the instrument into the exact spot on the left shoulder where it fits comfortably for that particular person. When that spot or "nest" is found, the head is turned left and the chin securely held down on the chin rest. The instrument must be aimed over the extended left foot to come into the "nest" at the correct angle and cover the shoulder properly. The teacher tries to keep up a fast pace because she finds this actually helps a child's accuracy. The teacher stands or kneels directly in front of the child for "Stop! Turn! Fly it in!" and then moves to the child's left as he turns his head left so his eyes will be "looking down the strings" for "Chin!"

3. Getting the violin from rest position to "Stop!" position requires that the child switch hands—the left hand comes down to take the violin ("baby") out of the right-hand "cradle."

4. The bow can be introduced very successfully through the use of child-sized paper cups. With his right (bow) hand, the child holds the cup full of pretend juice. He gets the "soft and round" feeling that the bow grip must have. Bow exercises can be done first with these cups. Elevators (straight up and down movement gathering speed after it can be done accurately at a slow pace), Stir the Pudding (a wide, circular movement to open up the arm), and Make a Breeze (out and in movement of the whole arm). Later, with the real bow, the child adds Windshield Wipers (a rotating movement of the lower arm in place at the child's side), Helicopters (bow held just above the top of the violin and moved very freely straight up and down—landing silently on a string), and Paint Rollers (circular arching rhythmical movements done as big as possible, with hands on either end of the bow). The child then tips the bow silently from string to string following the teacher's bow, to see if he can cross strings cleanly, "without a squeak." Doing this successfully means the child is beginning to get good bow control—not a grabbed, tight, scratch-producing grip, but a good balance of the hand on the bow.

5. Finding the exact spot where the child can hold his violin no hands

perfectly comfortably takes a while, and the teacher is willing to spend all the time on this that is necessary since it is such an important key to the child's playing comfort from this moment on.

6. The child holds his violin no hands to the count of five, ten, even twenty—the teacher stretching the time at each lesson.

7. The Get on Your Horse game done to the fourth rhythm is especially good for large muscle coordination, since the child must keep his feet still and only bend his knees to the music.

8. The teacher holds back on the bow as the child tries to pull the sound out of the string. This gives the child the feeling of resistance in the bow and "sinking into the string" that he needs for big tone. The teacher may also say something like, "Sticky bow sticks to the string," to give him that feeling. Suzuki says, "You don't play, the bow plays!"

9. When the children have all five *Twinkle* rhythms securely on open strings, the teacher has them face each other and touch left hands while they play. Later, when they're using fingering, the children can play *Twinkle* this way, touching left hands only when they come to open strings where their fingers aren't needed.

10. The children march around the room with pretend bows moving up and down to the rhythm played by the teacher.

11. A dowel is substituted for the bow and placed in the child's inside left elbow, his left arm raised as if playing the violin. In this way he can practice the "open up the elbow" feeling he needs in his bow arm without the encumbrance of the real instrument.

12. Two other ways to get the "open up your elbow" or "oil in your elbow" feeling involve no equipment whatsoever. In the first, the right hand moves lightly up and down the lower left arm ("wash your arm") with the easy broad movement required for good bowing. The second way is to pretend you're bouncing or dribbling a ball.

13. The teacher plays up and down a scale (A-Major, since that is the first key learned), the children "being" a scale with their bodies— from scrunched up on the floor to tiptoes and back down again.

14. When the children are finished playing they gently lower their violins to the floor "like falling leaves," and see if they can "touch down without a sound."

15. The children march around the room. When the music stops, they run back to their (manila folder) "feet."

16. The class ends with feet together—"kissing feet"—and a bow, to the slow and even count of "One . . . two . . . three." When we have an accompanist, we use: "Get ready chord" (dominant seventh) and "Bow chord" (tonic). The bow provides a neat beginning and ending to every class or performance, and it seems to give the children an extra grace, particularly at a concert.

A LIBRARY FOR PARENTS

With good reason, parents are crying out for help in finding their way as sensitively and intelligently as possible through the thoroughly confusing maze of conflicting advice about child-rearing coming at them from all directions. They become afraid to trust their own perfectly reliable gut reactions and, in wavering, begin the sad process of confusing their children through their own very understandable uncertainties. One day the mother of a nearly uncontrollable three-year-old whom I was having great difficulty teaching finally broke down in tears: "I have Ginott looking over one shoulder and Freud over the other. And next week I may read someone else who seems to know all there is to know about children. I have my own feelings about how to raise my child, but all this reading makes me doubt my way. Every week I try a new approach, and I seem to be bringing up a monster!"

I want to shout out loud and clear one strong and simple message to parents: You can, you *must* trust yourselves! Dr. Benjamin Spock, in an interview televised at our school, did a wonderful service for parents when he said no books can possibly serve as the last word—parents, the first and most important teachers of their children know *best* how to approach child-rearing. They must follow their own best judgment about raising their children, and use books only as references. He feels parents must listen to themselves first, and that what follows is far more natural than a regimen imposed from outside or taken too literally, no matter how erudite the "expert."

These books are recommended only as a supplement to the parent's own approach to his child; a means of checking a point here or affirming an action there. Some are purely inspirational— a superbly creative teacher, a philosophical view of the world as a place where all areas of learning can be naturally and beautifully integrated rather than fragmented and isolated, or exciting new research into the as yet little understood potential of infants. Others contain activities to share with a child and ways to make

his exposure to the world around him richer, and still others explore child, teacher, and parent development in ways that I feel
would be reassuring to parents.

When parents maintain or recapture the tremendous thirst
for learning they all had as very young children, there can be no
limit to the richness and naturalness of their experience with children. This bibliography is meant as an attempt to bring together
the best of our culture for children. The boundaries of exploration
into what can be done for very young children can be greatly extended by adults who truly become the rich resources for learning
that children need them to be.

Child-Teacher-Parent Development

Briggs, Dorothy Corkille. *Your Child's Self-Esteem*. New York: Doubleday, Dolphin Books, 1975.

A calm and warmly sensitive approach to child-rearing that is bound to
give strength and reassurance to parents. In her gentle way, Briggs reminds us that "living with your child so that he is deeply and quietly glad
that he is who he is gives him a priceless legacy; strength to meet stress,
and courage to become committed, responsible, productive, and creative—a
fully *human* person." This book about child development comes remarkably close to Suzuki's ideas.

Cohen, Dorothy. *The Learning Child*. New York: Random House, 1972.

One of the finest and most sensitive books about children's learning. It
deals with different stages of learning through the intermediate years and
states important conclusions about children coping with a troubled world
and the partnership between teacher and parent that is the key to their
success. "The capacity to love and the capacity to work make more sense
than ever in a push-button civilization so managed as to rob individuals
of their deepest sense of self as men and women of dignity."

———, and Virginia Stern. *Observing and Recording the Behavior of Young
Children*. New York: Teachers College Press, 1974.

I include this book to give parents an inside view into this most scientific
approach to studying children, so that they may learn some of its techniques and become more aware of their own children in doing so. This
is an exceptionally clear and helpful book—though precise in detail, its
language is simple and direct and its tone warm. Reading it, I believe,
will help parents by taking the mystery out of what teachers look for and
find in children's behavior.

Erikson, Erik. *Childhood and Society*. Second edition. New York: W.W. Norton Company, 1963.

Although definitely Freudian in slant, the book is written with an extraordinary warmth and breadth of human understanding. Particularly important is the section entitled "Eight Ages of Man." The author comes across clearly as a man and teacher uniquely perceptive about people and an unusually sensitive student of children. This is both science and poetry, and a delight to read.

Fraiberg, Selma *The Magic Years*. New York: Charles Scribner's Sons, 1959.

An excellent basic text for dealing with any problems that may arise in the very early years, from birth to six. Excellent for answering parents' specific questions about development and behavior. Intelligent and sensitive, with a chatty style, Fraiberg shows warmth and concern for children and seeks always to reassure parents.

Ginott, Haim. *Between Parent and Child*. New York: The Macmillan Company, 1965.

A very positive, down-to-earth approach to children that underlines a healthy relationship between child and parent by putting it on an entirely straightforward basis. Direct and honest communication is stressed in a way that has brought many parents relief in their search for ways to handle tough situations, particularly those that involve anger and potential stalemate in discussion. Practical, warm, and wise, this book shows parents many ways to use their own best judgment with children rather than make snap decisions based on a hasty reaction, out of anger or frustration.

Isaacs, Susan. *The Nursery Years*. New York: Schocken Books, 1968.

Concerned with the intellectual growth of the child from birth to six years, Isaacs notes, "I have no doubt that all of us greatly underestimate the intelligence and power of observation of young children—largely, perhaps, because it suits us to do so." She shows the importance of sensitivity and compassion in entering into the child's own world "with an informed sympathy," and seeks to enlist parents in keeping "exact and full records of the development of their own children" so that teachers and parents together can give children "things to do and play with which will feed their skill and power."

Jersild, Arthur. *When Teachers Face Themselves*. New York: Teachers College Press, 1955.

I include this book because I think it is important for parents to be as close as possible to a deep understanding of what it takes to be a good teacher. Most concern is given here to the teacher's being in tune with himself before he tries to become attuned to others, especially young children. Parents should know something of this self-search so that they come to know and appreciate teachers as human, and not as a race apart.

Landers, Ray. *The Talent Education School of Shinichi Suzuki: An Analysis*. Revised third edition. New York: Exposition, 1984.

Dr. Landers, a Suzuki piano teacher, has written a well-documented, intellectually stimulating book about the ideas of Shin'ichi Suzuki and their place in the world of education and thought at large. This is a refreshingly rich and detailed treatment, giving the history, philosophy, and method of Talent Education from the perspective of someone interested in the child's entire, not just musical, education. Landers concludes: "A system that offers hope to even the most slowly developing child raises great optimism for the growth and education of greater numbers of people. When encouraged by leaders as optimistic as Suzuki, Talent Education could benefit mankind greatly, just as it has already greatly influenced music education."

Moustakas, Clark. *The Authentic Teacher*. Cambridge, Massachusetts: Howard A. Doyle, 1966.

Although this sensitive, wise, and often poetic book was written with the purpose of encouraging in teachers the development of sensitivity and awareness in the classroom, it can encourage the very same qualities in parents as well. Written in a very straightforward style with an obvious and strong emotional commitment by the author, *The Authentic Teacher* really points beyond teachers to the need for authentic people. "The significant adult must exist for the growing individual as someone there, to be met, related to and affected by, as a real person whose very presence helps to evolve awareness and beauty, stimulates and challenges potentialities, and provides an opportunity for expansion of self in the aesthetic and spiritual realm, as well as in intellectual pursuits."

Slone, Kay Collier. *They're Rarely Too Young and Never Too Old to Twinkle*. Lexington, Kentucky: Life Force Press, 1982.

Kay Slone, an extraordinary Suzuki violin teacher and a person whose whole life joyfully reflects the Suzuki philosophy, has written one of the most lucid and warmly perceptive books about beginning Suzuki violin and the Suzuki philosophy. She is precise and clear in prescribing the step-by-step progression she follows in her very successful Suzuki teaching. One does not have to use all her ideas to find her book an enormous inspiration for teaching—and for parenting as well. She writes as she speaks, with warmth, perception, and absolute clarity: "We need to be aware of the need for being centered, balanced persons—and we need to start from the earliest days of our children's lives to help them become such persons."

Starr, William, and Constance Starr. *To Learn with Love*. Knoxville, Tennessee: Kingston Ellis, 1983.

This is a warmly down-to-earth book written by two of America's best-known Suzuki teachers, a violinist and a pianist who are also the parents of eight children! This volume is rightfully in demand among Suzuki parents. It is realistic, yet also idealistic and optimistic, encouraging parents to set their expectations for their children not too low yet not too high. Written from the point of view of both husband and wife, the book covers all aspects of Suzuki instruction in the context of the entire life of the family. Mrs. Starr ends the book with her own feelings about the Suzuki philosophy: "It is this celebration of life that is the magnet that draws people of all nations and creeds to Suzuki and his Talent Education. It is for this that we, parents and teachers, now and in the future, shall be eternally grateful to him." (The Starrs include an important chapter on nutrition, and a special bibliography to go with it.)

Books for Inspiration

Ashton-Warner, Sylvia. *Teacher*. New York: Simon and Schuster, 1963.

An extraordinarily moving account of one woman's experiences teaching Maori children in New Zealand—her inner searches are as important as the wonderfully creative curriculum she devised: the "key vocabulary" that "unlocks the mind and releases the tongue." This beautiful and lyrical book is a testament to what joy, love, compassion, wisdom, and intelligence can bring to children. It is as important for parents to read as for teachers.

Behrend, Louise. "Rosin in the Left Hand." New York: School for Strings, n.d.

A progress report covering the first six months of an experimental violin-teaching program, Suzuki based, sponsored by the Music School of the Henry Street Settlement in the pre-kindergarten classes at Manhattan's P.S. 134.

Bettelheim, Bruno. *The Uses of Enchantment*. New York: Random House, 1977.

The importance of fairy tales in a child's development—the way in which they allow a child, through their exaggerated characters, to play out emotions of his own through fantasy. Bettelheim decries the super-realists who insist it is harmful to tell children about Santa Claus because he is not real. He believes that presenting a child with "polarities of character . . . permits [him] to comprehend easily the difference between the two, which he could not do if the figures were true to life, with all the complexities that characterize real people." If the parent tells his child fairy-tales in the right spirit, the child feels "that he is not alone in his fantasy life—that it is shared by the person he needs and loves most. Under such favorable conditions, fairy tales communicate to the child an intuitive, subconscious understanding of his own nature and of what his future may hold if he develops his potential." A wonderful reminder for modern parents that they must not neglect to transmit our rich cultural heritage to children as it was transmitted to us, and a suggestion that if children are reared so that their lives are truly meaningful to them, they will not need special help.

Billings, Helen K. *How to Give Your Child a Priceless Educational Advantage at Home, Free.* Fort Lauderdale, Florida: Helen K. Billings Educational Foundation, 1976.

Dr. Billings has written a joyfully optimistic book about parents working with their own children, that reflects her lifelong and worldwide work with the philosophy and methods of Maria Montessori. This is an inspiring book for parents, enthusiastically written by a woman whose deep love of children and faith in their endless potential strikingly parallels Suzuki's. "We must have the attention, the cooperation, the willingness to participate in this largest of all our problems, How to help our children develop the qualities that make a healthy, happy, prosperous society that will set standards and provide leadership for countries all over the world."

Bland, Jane. *Art of the Young Child.* Third edition. New York: Museum of Modern Art, 1968.

A very clear explanation of the stages of children's artistic development, including many illustrations of this growth and a section on ways in which parents and teachers can encourage art expression in children. Written by a superb teacher of very young children, this book above all encourages acceptance and respect for what children create: "That child is lucky whose parents and teachers are as delighted with each forward step in the language of art as they are with each new venture in speech."

Bronowski, Jacob. *Science and Human Values.* New York: Harper and Row, 1956.

·A wise and poetic discussion of the ways in which science is as integral to our culture as the arts. Bronowski (*The Ascent of Man*) is a remarkable Renaissance man who sees all areas of learning inextricably integrated—he sees the science in the art and the art in the science. The book ends with a very amusing dialogue—"The Abacus and the Rose." The idea of "unity out of variety" is an important one for parents and teachers alike in this overspecialized world.

Cazden, Courtney. *Infant School.* Newton, Massachusetts: Education Development Center, 1969.

A very warm and informative interview with a British infant school teacher using, with particular effect, some of the approaches of the integrated day, a form of open classroom developed in England. There is an accompanying film made by Lillian Weber called *Infants School,* which includes the classroom described here. The interview is important for parents as well as teachers in that it provides an excellent picture of the thinking of a creative and intelligent teacher making the most of large numbers of children and limited space. This teacher's calm, practical wisdom seems to extend to her room and all its children with very favorable results.

Chukovsky, Kornei. *From Two to Five.* Berkeley: University of California Press, 1963.

Calling children "linguistic geniuses," Chukovsky marvels at the intellectual effort all children make in mastering their native tongue. His background is Russian, but the book is really about children everywhere. "In truth the young child is the hardest mental toiler on our planet." He "values knowledge above all else." Chukovsky is a poet himself, writes poetically and emotionally, and believes fervently that "the future belongs to those who do not rein in their imagination." Fantasy makes children "creative thinkers in any field." An important reminder of the richness poetry, nonsense verses, and fairy tales bring to children's lives, and of the inherent inventiveness in all children: all in all, a delightful book.

Doman, Glenn. *How to Teach Your Baby to Read.* New York: Random House, 1964.

I am including this book without having observed or tried out this approach myself. If successfully and humanely put into practice, Doman's ideas could have very exciting implications for the future of early education.

Featherstone, Joseph. *Informal Schools in Britain Today: An Introduction.* New York: Citation Press, 1971.

An excellent introduction to the work in "integrated day" techniques in Britain, with exciting implications for American education. (The British find it ironic that although they took their "integrated day" from our Progressive Movement of the thirties, we are now trying so hard to learn from what they have evolved from our pioneering.) Particularly interesting for American observers is the important combination of independence for teachers and strong support from supervisors.

Frederick, Lisa. *An Approach to Music Through Eurhythmics.* Boston: New England Conservatory, n.d.

This pamphlet is a succinct and beautifully expressive description of the importance of Eurhythmics in giving a child a sense of musical meter as an integral part of his body movements. "It is through his body's rhythms that [the child] can grasp the rhythms outside himself . . . Movement is the child's first, most instinctive response to music."

Grilli, Susan. "A Suzuki-Centered Pre-School Curriculum." Master's thesis. New York: Bank Street College of Education, 1976.

The program of The Suzuki Pre-School, including part of a case study, worksheets, Suzuki violin games, work with parents, and the rationale for this experiment in extending Suzuki's educational idea from music to other areas of learning. Based largely on the second year of work in this school.

Hermann, Evelyn. *Shinichi Suzuki: The Man and His Philosophy.* Athens, Ohio: Ability Development, 1981.

A biography of Dr. Suzuki written by a well-respected Suzuki violin teacher whose involvement with the Suzuki philosophy has led to becoming executive secretary of the International Suzuki Association. The book includes important sections on the Suzuki philosophy, its history, and many of Suzuki's own teaching points.

Hirsch, Elisabeth. *The Block Book.* Washington, D.C.: NAEYC, 1974.

This important book shows how all areas of learning can be enhanced for children through block building. There are special sections on block building as art, science, math, social studies, dramatic play. Many illustrations help parents and teachers understand how to choose blocks for children and what development to look for in the stages of children's block building. A fascinating book.

Holt, John. *How Children Fail.* New York: Pitman, 1964.

A revolutionary book when it first came out, *How Children Fail* shows very clearly how children's learning needs must be met. In the more than ten years since the book came out so strongly against most schools, Holt went from a man hopeful of change to one rather embittered about the lack of it. His most recent books have gone so far as to advocate parents' taking children out of school altogether if they want good education. What is important is the idea of observing children closely to see exactly how they learn and building curricula to suit children's actual needs. We have been paying lip service to this idea but very few parents and teachers have really followed through on it. Still an important book.

Honda, Masaaki. *Talent Education: A Program for Early Development.* Tokyo: Talent Education Early Development Association, n.d.

Written by a medical doctor whose children have studied with Suzuki and who now works largely with the handicapped, this booklet sets forth the experiment in Tokyo to extend Suzuki's principles to areas outside music. It devotes much space to the Talent Education approach to violin instruction and the philosophy behind it. Dr. Honda accompanies all Talent Education concert tours of children from Japan.

Kuroyanagi, Tetsuko. *Totto-Chan: The Little Girl at the Window.* Tokyo: Kodansha International, 1982.

A totally delightful and deeply moving account, by one of Japan's most popular entertainers, about a very special teacher. The story is set in prewar and wartime Japan and revolves around the extraordinarily creative ways in which one imaginative and sensitive *sensei* made life wonderful and exciting for his students. This is an elegy to Sosaku Kobayashi, and though set in Japan it has universal appeal.

Lewin, Roger, ed. *Child Alive!* New York: Doubleday, 1975.

A collection of articles by researchers, primarily in England and Scotland, concerning the incredible potential of newborn babies and their extraordinary learning capacity. These scientists feel the newborn has been grossly underestimated and that education of very young children may have to change radically in recognition of this. The newborn baby displays "inbuilt rhythms" that are a prelude to the intentional and deliberate signaling which leads to the acquisition of language. The very exciting film *Benjamin,* shown in the Nova series on public television, led me to write to the BBC to ask for more information on this research. *Child Alive!* details much of this research in a very readable way. It is a most important book for parents as well as teachers.

Lewis, Claudia. "Writing for Young Children." New York: Bank Street College of Education, 1975.

A very beautifully written, poetic account of the ways children are reached best through literature, by a superb teacher of teachers, Claudia Lewis, who has also written several fine children's books of her own. She is so closely attuned to children's total involvement with their senses that she has a very special understanding of how to write for them. But this paper is about far more than writing for children—it is about understanding children in general and appreciating their unique approach to the world. As such it is for anyone concerned with young children, and it is a delight to read.

Marshall, Sybil. *An Experiment in Education.* Cambridge, England: Cambridge University Press, 1970.

A uniquely creative teacher in England building an exciting curriculum around art which integrates all areas of learning in a particularly rich way. The "symphonic method" makes art the rich central core of a curriculum from which other "strands" such as reading flow. Most inspiring is her very creative use of Beethoven's Sixth Symphony as a theme connecting work in all areas of learning in the classroom. Illustrations of artwork from her children show it to be exceptionally concentrated and imaginative. This book is fully capable of inspiring parents as much as teachers—not to copy exactly her "method" but rather to evolve approaches to children's learning of their own that are equally creative and that develop just as gradually and naturally from observation of children themselves. Sybil Marshall puts into practice what she believes—that experience is far more important than "genetic inheritance" to a child's intelligence. Children's "curiosity, ingenuity, creative ability, and boundless energy, are tools employed to obtain such experience."

McKee, Paul. *Primer for Parents*. Boston: Houghton Mifflin Company, 1966.

A book which shows how a child learns to read by subjecting parents to a "language" which they have never before seen and must decode. Parents find it necessary to go through the same steps in decoding that their children face when they are learning to read English. Parents find that they need the same kinds of help that children need and gain a far greater appreciation of the task facing children.

Mills, Elizabeth, et al. *In the Suzuki Style: A Manual for Raising Musical Consciousness in Children*. Berkeley: Diablo Press, 1974.

Encouragement and advice for parents of Suzuki students. The book includes ways to engage children musically, musical games to play, effective methods for violin tuning, and reasons why musical training should start early.

———, ed. *The Suzuki Concept: An Introduction to a Successful Method for Early Music Education*. Berkeley: Diablo Press, 1973.

A most helpful book of readings on the Suzuki approach as geared toward American parents. Includes a most valuable section, "Advice to a New Mother," which many parents have found reassuring and useful.

Montessori, Maria. *Dr. Montessori's Own Handbook*. New York: Schocken Books, 1965.

A good, clearly stated explanation of the Montessori philosophy is followed by details of the method. Montessori believes the environment is all-important for learning and that a good teacher is a good observer of children. The method has a lot to offer, if followed flexibly. Important ideas are that children possess naturally "the very qualities which organized education is supposed to produce, but which the overly solicitous teacher only succeeds in eradicating"; that teachers are enablers of learning (they do not force it on a child); and that all spheres of human activity are made meaningful to a child through his successful mastery of any one activity.

Murton, Alice. *From Home to School.* Informal Schools in Britain Today. New York: Citation Press, 1971.

"The overall need, in schools for young children, is companionship of understanding adults of all ages and kinds, working in cooperation with the teacher, and ready to play their part in children's need to communicate, not only with their peers, but with adults of every age." This expresses very well what we would like for our own school. Other important ideas in this very useful booklet are that parents should be brought into school activities fully a year before their child is enrolled; that the child should make more and more frequent visits preceding the enrollment; and that admission should be staggered so that only a small number of children are new to the class at any one time. Some particularly interesting case histories are included, and the importance of parent involvement is underscored over and over again. Of first importance is "the introduction of parents to new ways of learning, to the true value of play, [and] to the carry-over of such experiences into the home."

Pines, Maya. "Head, Head Start." *The New York Times Magazine* (October 26, 1975).

This article marked the general introduction of the Brookline Early Education Project (BEEP) to the public. BEEP was a network of experts who were made available to parents on request, even before a baby's birth, to advise and assist them in the complex job of child rearing. Medical, psychiatric, and educational leaders were on the BEEP staff for the use of parents, and a center in Brookline was set up for parents to visit for discussions, and to make use of book and toy libraries and a preschool. BEEP believed parents are the most important teachers of children and helped them do the best possible job. Dr. Burton White of the Harvard Pre-School Project, who was also a consultant to BEEP, felt that if BEEP were successful, it would "lead to a total reevaluation of our educational priorities. We spend nothing on a child's most important years, when the foundations of his educational capacity are being set. Then we spend more and more as he grows older, when he needs it less and less."

Richardson, Elwyn S. *In the Early World.* New York: Random House, 1964.

The subtitle of this beautifully written, beautifully designed book is appropriately, *Discovering Art Through Crafts.* Here is yet another truly inspired teacher, again working in New Zealand, whose curriculum evolved directly from the needs of the children he teaches. At his school crafts of phenomenal workmanship have been created by children and have served as the core of a program, from which other areas were then naturally and richly explored. The children's poetry is as inspired as their art.

This is a wonderful story of a rare teacher working with children in a richly creative way, using much more imagination and many fewer material resources then usual.

Suzuki, Shin'ichi. *Nurtured by Love*. New York: Exposition Press, 1968.

A very inspiring and wise book by the founder of the Talent Education movement in Japan setting forth his philosophy, the history of his idea, and the method of putting it in practice for the teaching of the violin to very young children. There is a simplicity and deep understanding of child development in Suzuki's brilliant way of giving so much to children through his careful observation of the ways in which they learn best. He bases his method on the way in which all children learn their native language, through imitation, repetition, and refinement. He deeply believes all children have virtually unlimited potential for achievement. This book explains the ways Suzuki goes about building a high degree of skill for children in such a pleasant environment that the habit of delight in learning need never be lost and true creativity gained.

———. *Ability Development from Age Zero*. Athens, Ohio: Ability Development, 1981.

A wonderful book Suzuki has written for parents and teachers—perhaps more down-to-earth than his more idealistic *Nurtured by Love*. Feeling that "the fate of the child is in the hands of the parent," Suzuki says, "If this book becomes a light of hope for mothers who love their children and wish for them to grow up wonderfully, I could not be happier."

Wickes, Linda. *The Genius of Simplicity*. Princeton, New Jersey: Summy-Birchard, 1982.

This is a clear, concise, and most intelligently written rationale for the Suzuki philosophy and method. This slim volume is a thoughtful yet incisive analysis, and will likely win many previously skeptical educators over to the Suzuki approach to all early education. Wickes clearly proves Suzuki ideas are at home among the finest in the world of education. She quotes many educators who think along strikingly similar lines as Suzuki to prove her point. An excellent book for parents with questions about the method in relation to other educational philosophies.

Activities to Share with Children

Aronoff, Frances. *Music and Young Children*. New York: Holt, Rinehart, and Winston, 1969.

Baratta-Lorton, Mary. *Workjobs*. Menlo Park, California: Addison-Wesley, 1972.

———. *Workjobs for Parents*. Menlo Park, California: Addison-Wesley, 1972.

Biggs, Edith. *Mathematics for Younger Children*. Informal Schools in Britain Today. New York: Citation Press, 1971.

Braley, William, Geraldine Konicki, and Catherine Leedy. *Daily Sensorimotor Training Activities*. Freeport, New York: Educational Activities, Inc., 1968.

Chin, Susan. "Origami for Children." Master's thesis. New York: Bank Street College of Education, 1977.

Cobb, Vicki. *Science Experiments You Can Eat*. Philadelphia: Lippincott, 1972.

Elementary Science Study. *The Musical Instrument Recipe Book*. Newton, Massachusetts: Education Development Center, 1968.

Findlay, Elsa. *Rhythm and Movement*. Evanston, Illinois: Summy-Birchard, 1971.

Glazer, Tom. *Eve Winker, Tom Tinker, Chin Chopper: Fifty Musical Fingerplays*. Garden City: Doubleday, 1973.

Holt, Michael, and Zoltan Dienes. *Let's Play Math*. New York: Walker, 1973.

Jayne, Caroline. *String Figures*. New York: Dover, 1962.

Mayhew, Martin, and Cherille Mayhew. *Fun with Art*. Cheadle, Cheshire: James Galt, 1970.

Richards, Roy. *Ourselves*. London: Macdonald Educational, 1973.

Sakade, Florence. *Origami: Book One*. Rutland, Vermont: Tuttle, 1957.

Books to Read to Children

Aliki. *My Visit to the Dinosaurs*. New York: Thomas Crowell, 1969.

Anderson, Jack. *The Nutcracker Ballet*. New York: Mayflower, 1979.

Anderson, Lonzo. *Two Hundred Rabbits*. New York: Viking, 1968.

Anno, Mitsumasa. *Anno's Alphabet*. New York: Thomas Y. Crowell Co., 1974.

——. *Topsy-Turvies*. New York and Tokyo: Weatherhill, 1970.

——. *Upside-Downers*. New York and Tokyo: Weatherhill, 1971.

Arbuthnot, May. *The Arbuthnot Anthology of Children's Literature*. Glenview, Illinois: Scott Foresman and Co., 1961.

Arno, Ed. *The Gingerbread Man*. New York: Scholastic, 1967.

Bancroft, Henrietta. *Animals in Winter*. New York: Scholastic, 1963.

Barton, Byron. *Where's Al?* New York: The Seabury Press, 1972.

Batherman, Muriel. *Big and Small. Short and Tall*. New York: Scholastic, 1972.

Belting, Natalia. *The Sun is a Golden Earring*. New York: Holt, Rinehart, and Winston, 1962.

Bemelmans, Ludwig. *Madeline*. New York: Viking Press, 1939.

Beskow, Elsa. *Pelle's New Suit*. New York: Scholastic, 1972.

Birmingham, John. *Mr. Gumpy's Motor Car*. New York: Thomas Crowell, 1976.

——. *Mr. Gumpy's Outing*. New York: Holt, Rinehart, and Winston, 1970.

Bradbury, Lynne. *Colors and Shapes*. Loughborough: Ladybird, 1981.

——. *Tell Me the Time*. Loughborough: Ladybird, 1981.

Branley, Franklin. *The Big Dipper*. New York: Thomas Crowell, 1962.

——. *Oxygen Keeps You Alive*. New York: Thomas Crowell, 1971.

Bridwell, Norman. *The Cat and the Bird in the Hat*. New York: Scholastic, 1964.

Brown, Margaret Wise. *Goodnight Moon*. New York: Harper and Row, 1947.

——. *The Runaway Bunny*. New York: Harper and Row, 1942.

——. *Wait Til' the Moon is Full*. New York: Harper and Row, 1948.

——. *Where Have You Been?* New York: Hastings House, 1952.

Burton, Virginia Lee. *Mike Mulligan and His Steam Shovel*. Boston: Houghton Mifflin Co., 1939.

Carrick, Carol, and Donald Carrick. *Beach Bird*. New York: Dial, 1973.

Chappell, Warren. *Peter and the Wolf*. New York: Alfred A. Knopf, Inc., 1968.

Child, Lydia. *Over the River and Through the Woods*. New York: Coward McCann and Geoghegan, Inc., 1974.

Crews, Donald. *We Read: A to Z*. New York: Harper and Row, 1967.

deForest, Charlotte, and Keiko Hida. *The Prancing Pony*. New York and Tokyo: Walker/Weatherhill, 1967.

deRegniers, Beatrice Schenk. *May I Bring a Friend?* New York: Atheneum, 1964.

Dr. Seuss [Theodore Geisel]. *ABC*. New York: Random House, 1963.

——. *And to Think That I Saw It on Mulberry Street*. New York: Vanguard, 1937.

——. *Green Eggs and Ham*. New York: Random House, 1960.

Dunn, Judy. *The Little Rabbit*. New York: Random House, 1980.

Duvoisin, Roger. *The Crocodile in the Tree*. New York: Alfred A. Knopf, Inc., 1958.

——. *Petunia Beware*. New York: Alfred A. Knopf, Inc., 1973.

Emberley, Barbara. *Drummer Hoff*. Englewood Cliffs: Prentice-Hall, 1967.

——. *One Wide River to Cross*. Englewood Cliffs: Prentice-Hall, 1966.

Erickson, Phoebe. *Who's in the Mirror?* New York: Alfred A. Knopf, Inc., 1965.

Feelings, Muriel. *Moja Means One*. New York: Dial, 1971.

Flack, Marjorie. *Angus and the Ducks*. New York: Doubleday, 1930.

——. *The Story About Ping*. New York: Viking Press, 1933.

Freeman, Don. *Corduroy*. New York: Viking, 1968.

——. *Tilly Witch*. New York: Viking Press, 1969.

Freschet, Bernice. *Bear Mouse*. New York: Scholastic, 1973.

Futamata, Eigoro. *How Not to Catch a Mouse*. New York and Tokyo: Weatherhill, 1972.

G'ag, Wanda. *Millions of Cats*. New York: Coward, McCann, and Geoghegan, 1928.

Galdone, Paul. *The Little Red Hen*. New York: The Seabury Press, 1973.

Gauch, Patricia. *Christina Katerina and the Box*. New York: Coward, McCann, and Geoghegan, 1971.

Gergeley, Tibor. *Busy Day, Busy People*. New York: Random House, 1973.

Gerson, Mary-Joan. *Why the Sky is Far Away*. New York: Harcourt Brace Jovanovich, 1974.

Ginsburg, Mirra. *Mushroom in the Rain*. New York: The Macmillan Co., 1974.

Green Tiger Press. *Hanimals*. La Jolla, California: 1982.

Gross, Ruth. *What is That Alligator Saying?* New York: Hastings House, 1972.

Grundy, Lynn. *A is for Apple*. Loughborough: Ladybird, 1980.

——. *I Can Count*. Loughborough: Ladybird, 1980.

Hoban, Russell. *A Baby Sister for Frances*. New York: Harper and Row, 1964.

——. *Bread and Jam for Frances*. New York: Scholastic, 1964.

Hoban, Tana. *Circles, Triangles, and Squares*. New York: The Macmillan Co., 1974.

Hopkins, Lee. *By Myself*. New York: Thomas Crowell, 1980.

Hunia, Fran. *Billy Goats Gruff*. Loughborough: Ladybird, Read it Yourself, 1977.

——. *Hansel and Gretel*. Loughborough: Ladybird, Read it Yourself, 1978.

Iwasaki, Chihiro. *A New Baby is Coming to My House*. New York: McGraw-Hill Book Co., 1970.

Johnson, Elizabeth. *All Color Book of Horses*. London: Octopus, 1972.

Keats, Ezra Jack. *Dreams*. New York: Collier, 1974.

——. *Goggles*. New York: Collier, 1969.

——. *Little Drummer Boy*. New York: Collier, 1968.

——. *Louie*. New York: Scholastic, 1975.

——. *Peter's Chair*. New York: Harper and Row, 1967.

——. *Regards to the Man in the Moon*. New York: Four Winds, 1981.

——. *The Snowy Day*. New York: Viking Press, 1962.

——. *The Trip*. New York: Scholastic, 1978.

——. *Whistle for Willie*. New York: Viking, 1964.

Kent, Jack. *There's No Such Thing as a Dragon*. New York: Golden, 1975.

King, Tony. *The Moving Alphabet Book*. New York: G.P. Putnam's, 1982.

Kipling, Rudyard. *The Elephant's Child*. New York: CBS Records, 1968.

Klein, Leonore. *Only One Art*. New York: Hastings House, 1971.

Krasilovsky, Phyllis. *The Cow Who Fell in the Canal*. New York: Doubleday, 1953.

Krauss, Ruth. *The Carrot Seed*. New York: Harper and Row, 1945.

Leaf, Munro. *The Story of Ferdinand*. New York: Viking Press, 1936.

Lewis, Claudia. *When I Go to the Moon*. New York: The Macmillan Co., 1961.

Lewis, Richard. *In a Spring Garden*. New York: The Dial Press, 1965.

Lewis, Stephen. *Zoo City*. New York: Greenwillow, 1976.

Lionni, Leo. *Fish is Fish*. New York: Pantheon, 1970.

——. *Swimmy*. New York: Random House, 1963.

Littledale, Freya. *The Magic Fish*. New York: Scholastic, 1967.

Livermore, Elaine. *Find the Cat*. Boston: Houghton Mifflin Co., 1973.

Lobel, Arnold. *Frog and Toad Are Friends*. New York: Harper and Row, 1970.

———. *Frog and Toad Together*. New York: Harper and Row, 1971.

———. *Lucille*. New York: Harper and Row, 1964.

Lundgren, Astrid. *The Tomten and the Fox*. New York: Coward McCann and Geoghegan, 1966.

Luzzati, Emanuele. *The Magic Flute*. New York: Scroll Press, Inc., 1973.

MacAgy, Douglas, and Elizabeth MacAgy. *Going for a Walk with a Line*. New York: Doubleday, 1959.

Margolis, Richard. *Only the Moon and Me*. Philadelphia: J.B. Lippincott and Co., 1969.

Matsuno, Masako. *Taro and the Bamboo Shoot*. New York: Random House, 1974.

Mayer, Mercer. *A Boy, A Dog, and A Frog*. New York: The Dial Press, 1967.

———. *Frog, Where Are You?* New York: The Dial Press, 1969.

McCloskey, Robert. *Make Way for Ducklings*. New York: Viking, 1941.

McMillan, Bruce. *The Alphabet Symphony*. New York: Greenwillow, 1977.

Merrill, Claire. *A Seed is a Promise*. New York: Scholastic, 1973.

Miles, Betty. *A Day of Autumn*. New York: Alfred A. Knopf, Inc., 1967.

Milne, A.A. *Now We Are Six*. New York: Dell, 1927.

———. *When We Were Very Young*. New York: Dell, 1924.

———. *Winnie the Pooh*. New York: Dell, 1926.

Minarik, Else. *Father Bear Comes Home*. New York: Harper and Row, 1959.

Montresor, Beni. *Cinderella*. New York: Alfred A. Knopf, Inc., 1965.

Moore, Clement. *A Visit from St. Nicholas*. New York: Wanderer, 1848.

Morris, Robert. *Dolphin*. New York: Scholastic, 1975.

Mosel, Arlene. *Tikki, Tikki, Tembo*. New York: Scholastic, 1968.

Nikly, Michelle. *The Emperor's Plum Tree*. New York: Greenwillow, 1982.

Parish, Peggy, *Amelia Bedelia*. New York: Scholastic, 1963.

Peppe, Rodney. *Cat and Mouse*. New York: Holt, Rinehart, and Winston, 1973.

Pinkwater, Daniel. *The Big Orange Splot*. New York: Scholastic, 1977.

Piper, Watty, *The Little Engine That Could*. New York: Platt and Munk, 1951.

Posell, Elsa. *This is an Orchestra*. Boston: Houghton Mifflin, 1973.

Potter, Beatrix. *The Tale of Jemima Puddle-Duck*. New York: Frederick Warne and Co., 1908.

———. *The Tale of Peter Rabbit*. New York: Dover Publications, Inc., 1972.

Preston, Edna. *Squawk to the Moon, Little Goose*. New York: Viking, 1974.

Provenson, Alice, and Martin Provenson. *A Child's Garden of Verses*. New York: Golden, 1951.

Random House Mother Goose, The. New York, 1949.

Reid, Alastair. *To Be Alive.* New York: Macmillan, 1966.

Rey, H.A. *Curious George Learns the Alphabet.* Boston: Houghton Mifflin Co., 1963.

——. *Curious George Rides a Bike.* Boston: Houghton Mifflin Co., 1952.

——. *Curious George Takes a Job.* Boston: Houghton Mifflin Co., 1947.

Rice, Eve. *Oh, Lewis.* New York: The Macmillan Co., 1974.

Rojankovsky, Feodor. *The Tall Book of Mother Goose.* New York: Harper and Row, 1942.

——. *The Tall Book of Nursery Tales.* New York: Harper and Row, 1944.

Sasek, M. *This is New York.* New York: Collier, 1960.

Sawyer, Ruth. *Journey Cake, Ho!* New York: Viking Press, 1953.

Scarry, Richard. *Best Word Book Ever.* New York: Golden Press, 1963.

Schaaf, Peter. *The Violin Up Close.* New York: Four Winds, 1980.

Sendak, Maurice. *Chicken Soup with Rice.* New York: Scholastic, 1962

——. *Where the Wild Things Are.* New York: Scholastic, 1963.

Sheehan, Angela. *The Squirrel.* London: Angus and Robertson, 1976.

Shulevitz, Uri. *One Monday Morning.* New York: Charles Scribner's Sons, 1967.

Simon, Seymour. *The Paper Airplane Book.* New York: Viking Press, 1971.

Slepian, Jan, and Ann Seidler. *The Hungry Thing.* New York: Scholastic, 1967.

Southgate, Vera. *The Elves and the Shoemaker.* Loughborough: Ladybird, Easy Reading, 1965.

——. *Goldilocks and the Three Bears.* Loughborough: Ladybird, Easy Reading, 1971.

Spier, Peter. *The Erie Canal.* New York: Doubleday, 1970.

——. *Noah's Flood.* New York: Doubleday, 1977.

Steig, William. *Amos and Boris.* New York: Farrar, Straus and Giroux, 1971.

——. *Sylvester and the Magic Pebble.* New York: E.P. Dutton, 1969.

Steiner, Charlotte. *My Slippers Are Red.* New York: Alfred A. Knopf, Inc., 1973.

Sugita, Yutaka. *1-2-3 Good-night!* Tokyo: Shikosha Publishing Co., 1972.

Suyeoka, George. *Momotaro.* Norfolk Island, Australia: Island Heritage, 1972.

Swift, Hildegarde. *The Little Red Lighthouse and the Great Gray Bridge.* New York: Harcourt Brace Jovanovich, 1942.

Thaler, Mike. *Penny Pencil.* New York: Harper and Row, 1963.

Turkle, Brinton. *Thy Friend, Obadiah.* New York: Viking, 1969.

Unesco. *Folk Tales from Asia, Book I.* New York, Tokyo: Weatherhill, 1975.

Voight, Ezra. *Peter and the Wolf*. Boston: David Godine, 1979.

Waber, Bernard. *Lyle, Lyle Crocodile*. Boston: Houghton Mifflin Co., 1965.

Wiesner, William. *Tom Thumb*. New York: Henry Z. Walck, Inc., 1974.

Withers, Carl. *The Tale of a Black Cat*. New York: Holt, Rinehart, and Winston, 1966.

Yashima, Taro. *Crow Boy*. New York: Viking Press, 1955.

Yeomans, John, and Quentin Blake. *The Bear's Water Picnic*. New York: The Macmillan Co., 1970.

Yoshikatsu, photographer. *Cat*. Tokyo: Shikosha, 1972.

———. *Puppy*. Tokyo: Shikosha, 1972.

BIBLIOGRAPHY

The sources listed below have been categorized into Suzuki-related materials, books and articles on education in general, and how-to books that provide concrete ideas and suggestions for teaching and learning activities. Some titles have been included in more than one category and may be found in the annotated Library for Parents as well. In addition to the materials listed below, three journals that reflect current writing about the Suzuki method and its application the world over that deserve note:

The Suzuki Journal. Edited by Robert Reinsager. Published by the Suzuki Association of the Americas, Box 354, Muscatine, Iowa 52761.

Suzuki World. Edited by Lorraine Fink. Published by Ability Development Associates, Inc., 79 East State Street, Athens, Ohio 45701.

Talent Education Journal. Edited by Masayoshi and Eiko Kataoka and translated by Kyoko Selden. Published by Talent Education of St. Louis, 236 Spring Avenue, St. Louis, Missouri 63119.

Suzuki-related Materials

Behrend, Louise. "No Shortage of String Players in Japan." New York: School for Strings, n.d.

———. "Rosin in the Left Hand." New York: School for Strings, n.d.

Cook, Clifford. *Suzuki Education in Action.* New York: Exposition Press, 1970.

Doman, Glenn. *How to Teach Your Baby to Read.* New York: Random House, 1964.

Edmunds, Sylvia. "A Parents' Manual for Little Fiddlers." Harwich, Massachusetts: Little Fiddlers Corporation, 1975.

———. "Project Little Fiddlers." Harwich, Massachusetts: Town of Harwich Public Schools, 1967.

Fink, Lorraine. *A Parent's Guide to String Instrument Study.* San Diego: KJOS, 1977.

Grilli, Susan. "Bunraku at Suzuki Pre-School." *American Suzuki Journal* 11:5 (September-October 1983).

———. "First Suzuki Pre-School Teachers' Workshop." *American Suzuki Journal* 12:3 (May-June 1984).

———. "The Pre-School Column." *American Suzuki Journal* 11:3 (April 1983).

———. "The Suzuki Pre-School: A Progress Report." *American Suzuki Journal* 10:5 (Fall 1982).

———. "The Suzuki Pre-School: Reflections on the First Ten Years." *American Suzuki Journal* 13:6 (November-December 1985).

———. "The Suzuki Pre-School: Toward a Civilized Future." *American*

Suzuki Journal 12:4 (July-August 1984) and 12:6 (November-December 1984).

——. "Suzuki Pre-School in New York City." *American Suzuki Journal* 6:3 (May 1978).

——. "Teacher-Training Unit 'A-P.'" *American Suzuki Journal* 12:1 (January-February 1984).

Grunes, Willa. "A Psychologist Looks at Suzuki Method." *American Suzuki Journal* 3:3 (Fall 1975).

Hermann, Evelyn. *Shinichi Suzuki: The Man and His Philosophy*. Athens, Ohio: Ability Development, 1981.

Honda, Masaaki. *Suzuki Changed My Life*. Evanston, Illinois: Summy-Birchard, 1976.

——. *Talent Education: A Program for Early Development*. Tokyo: Talent Education Early Development Association, n.d.

Ibuka, Masaru. *Kindergarten is Too Late*. New York: Simon and Schuster, 1977.

Johnson, Robert Leland. *Super Babies*. New York: Exposition, 1982.

Kendall, John. "Observation and Report." Carbondale: Southern Illinois University, 1959.

——. "The Resurgent String Program in America." *Music Educators Journal* (September-October 1967).

——. *The Suzuki Violin Method in American Music Education*. Washington, D.C.: MENC, 1978.

——. *The Suzuki Violin Method in American Music Education: What the American Music Educator Should Know About Shinichi Suzuki*. Washington, D.C.: MENC, 1973.

——. *Talent Education: The Violin Teaching Methods of Mr. Shinichi Suzuki*. Revised edition. Edwardsville, Illinois: Southern Illinois University, 1964.

——. *Talent Education and Suzuki*. Washington, D.C.: MENC, 1966.

——. *Today's Youth and the Violin: A Trilogy on Talent Education*. Lincolnwood, Illinois: William Lewis and Son, 1971.

——. "Violin Teaching for Three Year-Olds: Ten Stereotypes Reexamined." *Instrumentalist* (March 1960).

Landers, Ray. *The Talent Education School of Shinichi Suzuki: An Analysis*. Revised third edition. New York: Exposition Press, 1984.

Mills, Elizabeth, et al. *In the Suzuki Style: A Manual for Raising Musical Consciousness in Children*. Berkeley: Diablo Press, 1974.

——, ed. *The Suzuki Concept: An Introduction to a Successful Method for Early Music Education*. Berkeley: Diablo Press, 1973.

Paul, Anthony. "Music is Child's Play for Professor Suzuki." *Reader's Digest* (November 1973).

Slone, Kay Collier. *They're Rarely Too Young and Never Too Old to Twinkle*. Lexington, Kentucky: Life Force Press, 1982.

Starr, William. "Group Lessons." *American Suzuki Journal* 3:2 (Summer 1975).

——, and Constance Starr. *To Learn with Love*. Knoxville, Tennessee: Kingston Ellis Press, 1983.

——. *The Suzuki Violinist*. Knoxville, Tennessee: Kingston Ellis Press, 1976.

Suzuki, Shin'ichi. *Ability Development From Age Zero*. Athens, Ohio: Ability Development, 1981.

——. *Ability is Not Inherited*. Matsumoto, Japan: Talent Education Institute, n.d.

——. *The Law of Ability and the "Mother Tongue" Method of Education*. Excerpts of a talk given to the Japan Institute of Educational Psychology. Matsumoto, Japan: Talent Education Institute, October 1973.

——. *Nurtured by Love*. New York: Exposition Press, 1969.

——. *Suzuki Violin School, Volume 1* (Violin Part). Revised edition. Princeton, N.J.: Birch Tree Group Ltd. (Copyright 1978 by Zen-On Music Co., Ltd., Tokyo, Japan).

——. *Talent Education for Young Children*. New Albany, Indiana: World-Wide Press, 1986.

——. *Where Love is Deep*. Talent Education Journal: St. Louis, Missouri, 1982.

Van Sickle, Howard. "Talent Education Supported by Learning Theory." *Talent Education News* 1 (May-June 1969).

Wickes, Linda. *The Genius of Simplicity*. Princeton, New Jersey: Summy-Birchard, 1982.

Yurko, Michiko. *No H in Snake*. Sherman Oaks, California: Alfred, 1978.

General Education Materials

Aronoff, Frances. *Music and Young Children*. New York: Holt, Rinehart, and Winston, Inc., 1969.

Ashton-Warner, Sylvia. *Teacher*. New York: Simon and Schuster, 1963.

Baby Talk. In the *Nova* series, WGBH TV. Televised February 26, 1985.

Baker, Russell. *Growing Up*. New York: Congdon and Weed, 1982.

Barth, Roland, and Charles Rathbone. *A Bibliography of Open Education*. Newton, Massachusetts: Advisory for Open Education and Education Development Center, 1971.

Baruch, Dorothy. *One Little Boy*. New York: Delta, 1952.

Benjamin. In the *Nova* series. WGBH TV. Televised May 9, 1976.

Bettelheim, Bruno, and Karen Zelan. *On Learning to Read*. New York: Vintage/Random House, 1982.

Bettelheim, Bruno. "The Uses of Enchantment." *The New Yorker* (December 8, 1975).

Biber, Barbara. *Children's Drawings: From Lines to Pictures*. New York: Bank Street College of Education, reissued 1967.

———, et al. *Promoting Cognitive Growth: A Developmental Interaction Point of View*. New York: Bank Street College of Education, 1971.

Biggs, Edith, and James MacLean. *Freedom to Learn*. Don Mills, Ontario: Addison-Wesley of Canada, 1969.

Billings, Helen. *How to Give Your Child a Priceless Educational Advantage at Home, Free*. Fort Lauderdale, Florida: The Helen K. Billings Educational Foundation, 1976.

Blackie, John. *Inside the Primary School*. New York: Schocken, 1971.

Bland, Jane. *Art of the Young Child*. New York: Museum of Modern Art, 1968.

Blitz, Barbara. *The Open Classroom: Making It Work*. Boston: Allyn and Bacon, 1973.

Brearly, Molly, et al. *Educating Teachers*. Informal Schools in Britain Today. New York: Citation, 1972.

———. *The Teaching of Young Children*. New York: Schocken, 1970.

Briggs, Dorothy Corkille. *Your Child's Self-Esteem*. New York: Dolphin/Doubleday, 1975.

Bronowski, Jacob. *Science and Human Values*. New York: Harper and Row, 1956.

Brookline Early Education Project. *Progress Reports and Infant-Toddler Curriculum*. Brookline, Massachusetts: BEEP, 1974, 1975.

Brown, Mary, and Norman Precious. *The Integrated Day in the Primary School*. London: Ward Lock Educational, 1968.

Bruner, Jerome. *Under Five in Great Britain*. Ypsilanti, Michigan: High/Scope Press, 1980.

Carnegie Forum on Education and the Economy: *A Nation Prepared: Teachers for the Twenty-first Century* (The Report of the Task Force on Teaching as a Profession). New York: May 1986.

Cazden, Courtney. *Infant School*. Newton, Massachusetts: Education Development Center, 1969.

Child's Play. In the *Nova* series, WGBH TV. Televised March 12, 1985.

Choksy, Lois. *The Kodaly Method*. Englewood Cliffs, New Jersey: Prentice-Hall, Inc., 1974.

Chukovsky, Kornei. *From Two to Five*. Berkeley: University of California Press, 1963.

Cohen, Dorothy. *The Learning Child*. New York: Random House, 1972.

——, and Virginia Stern. *Observing and Recording the Behavior of Young Children*. New York: Teachers College Press, Columbia University, 1958.

Dalcroze, Emile-Jacques. *Rhythm, Music, and Education*. Geneva: The Dalcroze Society, 1973.

Developing Child, The (Part I). In the *Innovation* series, WNET TV, No. 225. Televised May 31, 1984.

Early Development Association. *International Symposium in Early Childhood Development*. Tokyo: Early Development Association, 1979.

Elbow, Peter, *Writing Without Teachers*. London: Oxford University Press, 1973.

Erikson, Erik. *Childhood and Society*. Revised edition. New York: W.W. Norton and Co., 1963.

Farber, M.A. "Project Teaches Parents Use of Educational Toys." *The New York Times* (March 30, 1970).

Featherstone, Joseph. *An Introduction*. Informal Schools in Britain Today. New York: Citation Press, 1971.

Fiske, Edward. "Carnegie Panel Plans to Establish Nationwide Teacher Certification." *The New York Times* (May 16, 1986).

Fraiberg, Selma. *The Magic Years*. New York: Charles Scribner's Sons, 1959.

Gardner, John W. *Excellence*. Revised edition. New York: W.W. Norton, 1984.

Gattegno, Caleb. *What We Owe Children*. New York: Avon, 1971.

Gelb, Barbara. "Pied Piper of Dance." *The New York Times Magazine* (April 12, 1981).

Ginott, Haim. *Between Parent and Child*. New York: The Macmillan Company, 1965.

Gordon, Thomas. *Parent Effectiveness Training*. New York: Wyden, 1975.

Grilli, Susan. "A Suzuki-Centered Pre-School Curriculum." Master's thesis. New York: Bank Street College of Education, 1976.

Hartley, Ruth, et al. *Understanding Children's Play*. New York: Columbia University Press, 1952.

Hechinger, Fred. "Harsh Charges Against Computers." *The New York Times* (July 10, 1984).

——. "How Do Children Learn to Write?" *The New York Times* (November 30, 1982).

——. "Nature vs. Nurture: Psychologist Urges Active Intervention." *The New York Times* (March 24, 1981).

——. "Teachers Now Seek Parental Participation." *The New York Times* (November 20, 1979).

Hirsch, Elisabeth. *The Block Book*. Washington, D.C.: NAEYC, 1974.

Holt, John. *How Children Fail*. New York: Pitman, 1964.

——. *How Children Learn*. New York: Dell, 1983.

Hymes, James. *The Child Under Six*. Englewood Cliffs, New Jersey: Prentice-Hall, 1961.

I.D.E.A. *Early Childhood Series: The British Infant School*. Melbourne, Florida: Institute for the Development of Educational Activities, Inc., 1969.

Isaacs, Susan. *The Nursery Years*. New York: Schocken Books, 1968.

Jersild, Arthur. *When Teachers Face Themselves*. New York: Teachers College Press, 1955.

Keller, Wilhelm. *Orff Schulwerk*. London: Schott, 1963.

Keniston, Kenneth. *All Our Children*. New York: Harvest/Harcourt Brace Jovanovich, 1977.

——. "The MacNeil-Lehrer Report," WNET TV, September 13, 1977.

Koch, Kenneth. *Rose, Where Did You Get That Red?* New York: Vintage/Random House, 1973.

Kohl, Herbert. *Growing With Your Children*. Boston: Little, Brown, 1978.

——. *The Open Classroom*. New York: Random House, 1969.

Kreisberg, Luisa. "Art for Math's Sake." In the education supplement of *The New York Times* (April 25, 1976).

Kuroyanagi, Tetsuko. *Totto-Chan: The Little Girl at the Window*. Tokyo: Kodansha International, 1982.

Leonard, George. *Education and Ecstasy*. New York: Delta, 1968.

Lewin, Roger, et al. *Child Alive!* New York: Doubleday, 1975.

Lewis, Claudia. *Writing for Young Children*. New York: Bank Street College of Education, 1954.

MacLaine, Shirley. *Out on a Limb*. New York: Bantam Books, 1983.

Maeroff, Gene. "Classical Music Not Their Thing." *The New York Times* (December 4, 1984).

——. "Special Education in Regular Classes." *The New York Times* (December 11, 1979).

Marshall, Sybil. *An Experiment in Education*. Cambridge, England: Cambridge University Press, 1970.

McKee, Paul. *Primer for Parents*. Boston: Houghton Mifflin, 1966.

Montessori, Maria. *Dr. Montessori's Own Handbook*. New York: Schocken Books, 1965.

Moustakas, Clark. *The Authentic Teacher*. Cambridge, Massachusetts: Howard A. Doyle, 1966.

Murton, Alice. *From Home to School*. Informal Schools in Britain Today. New York: Citation, 1971.

Naiman, Adeline, Courtney Cazden, and Nancy Weston. *Infant School.* Newton, Massachusetts: Education Development Center, 1969.

National Commission for Excellence in Education. *A Nation at Risk: The Imperative for Educational Reform.* Washington, D.C.: U.S. Department of Education, April 1983.

Neill, A.S. *Freedom, Not License!* New York: Hart, 1966.

Neugebauer, Roger, and Robert Lurie. *Caring for Infants and Toddlers: What Works, What Doesn't.* Summit, New Jersey: Summit Child Care Center, 1980.

Pierson, Donald, and Mary Jane Yurchak. "Brookline Early Education Project: One Model for an Early Start." *Top of the News,* November, 1974.

——. *The Second Year of the Brookline Early Education Project.* Brookline, Massachusetts: Brookline Early Education Project (BEEP), October 31, 1974.

Pifer, Alan. "Children—A National Resource." Speech given to Conference of Child Welfare League, reprinted in *High/Scope Resource* 2:2 (October 1982). Ypsilanti, Michigan: High/Scope Educational Research Foundation.

Pines, Maya. "Head, Head Start." *The New York Times Magazine* (October 26, 1975).

——. *Revolution in Learning: The Years From Birth to Six.* New York: Harper and Row, 1967.

——. "What Produces Great Skills? Specific Pattern is Discerned." *The New York Times* (March 30, 1982).

Pirsig, Robert. *Zen and the Art of Motorcycle Maintenance.* New York: Bantam, 1974.

Richardson, Elwyn. *In the Early World.* New York: Random House, 1964.

Rockefeller, David Jr. "Wanted: A New Policy for the Arts in Education." *The New York Times* (May 22, 1977).

Rogers, Fred. "Nurturing Creative Energy." *The New York Times Magazine* (August 21, 1983).

Schweinhart, L.J., and D.P. Weikart. *Young Children Grow Up: The Effects of the Perry Pre-School Project on Youths Through Age 15.* Ypsilanti, Michigan: High/Scope Press, 1980.

Travers, P.L. "I Never Wrote for Children." *The New York Times Magazine* (July 2, 1978).

Tsurumi, Yoshi. "Credibility Gap in School." Editorial in *The New York Times* (May 2, 1983).

Tuchman, Barbara. "The Decline of Quality." *The New York Times Magazine* (November 2, 1980).

Weber, Lillian. *The English Infant School and Informal Education.* Englewood Cliffs: Prentice-Hall, 1971.

Weinraub, Judith. "New British Study on Education Says Old Way is Best Way." *The New York Times* (May 8, 1976).

White, Burton. Publications of The Center for Parent Education, Cambridge, Massachusetts.

White, Merry. "Japanese Education: How Do They Do It?" In *Japan Society Newsletter* 32:2 (September 1984).

——. *The Japanese Educational Challenge: A Commitment to Children.* New York: The Free Press, 1987.

Wilkins, Joan. *Breaking the T.V. Habit.* New York: Charles Scribner's Sons, 1982.

Winn, Marie. "The Loss of Childhood." *The New York Times Magazine* (May 8, 1983).

——. "What Became of Childhood Innocence?" *The New York Times Magazine* (January 25, 1981).

How-To Books and Resources

Arnold, Leona. *Ideas for Putting a Day Care Classroom Together and Things to Make and Do With Children* (from *Manual on Organization of Day Care Centers,* second edition). New York: Bank St. College of Education, 1971.

Aschiem, Skip, ed. *Materials for the Open Classroom.* New York: Delacorte Press/Seymour Lawrence, 1971.

Association of Childhood Education International. *Bits and Pieces.* Washington, D.C.: Association of Childhood Education International, 1967.

——. *Nursery School Portfolio.* Washington, D.C.: Association of Childhood Education International, 1969.

Baratta-Lorton, Mary. *Workjobs.* Menlo Park, California: Addison-Wesley, 1972.

Biggs, Edith. *Mathematics for Younger Children.* Informal Schools in Britain Today. New York: Citation, 1971.

Braley, William, Geraldine Konicki, and Catherine Leedy. *Daily Sensorimotor Training Activities.* New York: Educational Activities, Inc., 1968.

Caney, Steven. *The Toy Book.* New York: Workman Publishing Co., 1972.

Cherry, Clare, and Lear Sigler. *Creative Art of the Developing Child.* Belmont, California: Fearon Publishers, 1972.

Chin, Susan. "Origami for Children, Developmentally From Ages Six to Eleven." Master's thesis. New York: Bank St. College of Education, 1977.

Cobb, Vicki. *Science Experiments You Can Eat.* Philadelphia: J.B. Lippincott Co., 1972.

Collins, John B. *Starting Points in Art.* London: Ward Lock Educational, 1969.

d'Amboise, Jacques, Hope Cooke, and Carolyn George. *Teaching the Magic of Dance.* New York: Simon and Schuster, 1983.

Early Childhood Education Study. *Materials: A Useful List of Classroom Items That Can Be Scrounged or Purchased*. Newton, Massachusetts: Education Development Center, n.d.

———. *Single Sheets*. Newton, Massachusetts: Education Development Center, n.d.

Education Development Center. *A Classroom for Young Children: Approximation* #1. Newton, Massachusetts.: Education Development Center, 1971.

———. *Introduction to the Elementary Science Study*. Newton, Massachusetts.: Education Development Center, 1966.

Edwards, Betty. *Drawing on the Right Side of the Brain*. Los Angeles: J.P. Tarcher, 1979.

Elementary Science Study of the Education Development Center. *Children Printing*. Newton, Massachusetts: Education Development Center, 1969.

———. *Match and Measure: A Working Paper*. Newton, Massachusetts: Education Development Center, 1969.

———. *The Musical Instrument Recipe Book*. Newton, Massachusetts: Education Development Center, 1968.

———. *Primary Balancing*. New York: McGraw-Hill, 1976.

———. *Sink or Float*. Newton, Massachusetts: Education Development Center, 1968.

———. *Tracks and Track Picture Book*. Newton, Massachusetts: Education Development Center, 1968.

———. *Whistles and Strings*. Newton, Massachusetts: Education Development Center, 1968.

Engel, Brenda. *Arranging the Informal Classroom*. Newton, Massachusetts: Education Development Center, 1973.

Findlay, Elsa. *Rhythm and Movement: Applications of Dalcroze Eurhythmics*. Evanston, Illinois: Summy-Birchard Company, 1971.

Follow-Through. *A Classroom for Young Children: Approximation*. Newton, Massachusetts: Education Development Center, 1971.

Fournier, Raymond, and Vincent Presno. *Advantage*. Englewood Cliffs, New Jersey: Prentice-Hall, Inc., 1965.

Frederick, Lisa. *An Approach to Music Through Eurhythmics*. Boston: New England Conservatory, n.d.

Glazer, Tom. *Eye Winker, Tom Tinker, Chin Chopper: Fifty Musical Fingerplays*. Garden City, New York: Doubleday Publishers, 1973.

Her Majesty's Stationery Office, Department of Education and Science. *Movement: Physical Education in the Primary Years*. London: Her Majesty's Stationery Office, 1970.

Holt, Michael, and Zoltan Dienes. *Let's Play Math*. New York: Walker, 1973.

Hoover, F. Louis. *Art Activities for the Very Young*. Worcester, Massachusetts: Davis Publications, Inc., 1961.

Jacob, Stacie, ed. *Manual on Organization, Financing, and Administration of Day Care Centers in New York City for Community Groups, Their Lawyers, and Other Advisors*. Second edition. New York: Bank Street College of Education, 1971.

Jayne, Caroline. *String Figures and How to Make Them*. New York: Dover Publications, Inc., 1962.

Landeck, Beatrice. *Songs to Grow On*. New York: Marks and Sloane, 1950.

Leitman, Allan, and Cornelia Voorhees. *Moments in Learning*. Newton, Massachusetts: Education Development Center, 1968.

——. and Edith Churchill. *A Classroom for Young Children*. Newton, Massachusetts: Education Development Center, 1966.

May, Dorothy. *Suggestions for Play Activities for Young Children*. London: Save the Children Fund, 1967.

May, Marian, ed. *Crafts for Children*. Menlo Park, California: Lane Books, Sunset Series, 1971.

Mayhew, Martin, and Cherille Mayhew. *Fun with Art*. Cheadle, Cheshire, England: Galt and Co., 1970.

Miller, Mary, and Paula Zajan. *Finger Play*. New York: G. Schirmer, 1955.

Monahan, Robert. *Free and Inexpensive Materials for Pre-School and Early Childhood*. Belmont, California: Fearon, 1973.

Nuffield Mathematics Project. *Beginnings*. Edinburgh: Nuffield Foundation, 1967.

——. *I Do and I Understand*. Edinburgh: Nuffield Foundation, 1967.

——. *Mathematics Begins*. Edinburgh: Nuffield Foundation, 1967.

Nursery School Association of Great Britain and Northern Ireland. *Making Musical Apparatus and Instruments, 71*. London: Nursery School Association of Great Britain and Northern Ireland, 1957.

Pile, Naomi. *Art Experiences for Young Children*. New York: The Macmillan Co., Threshold Division, 1972.

Project Head Start. *Beautiful Junk*. Washington, D.C.: Office of Child Development, U.S. Department of Health, Education, and Welfare, 1973.

Reichard, Cary, and Dennis Blackburn. *Music-Based Instruction for the Exceptional Child*. Denver, Colorado: Love Publishing Co., 1973.

Richards, Roy, *Ourselves*. London: MacDonald Educational, 1973.

Rippy, Rachel, ed. *Finding and Using Scrounge Materials*. Washington, D.C.: Office of Education, U.S. Department of Health, Education, and Welfare, 1975.

Ross, Laura, and Frank Ross Jr. *Finger Puppets*. New York: Lee and Shepard Co., 1971.

Sakade, Florence. *Origami: Book I.* Rutland, Vermont: Charles Tuttle Co., 1957.

Sargent, Betsye. *The Integrated Day in an American School*. Boston: The National Association of Independent Schools, 1970.

Simon, Henry. *A Treasury of Christmas Songs and Carols*. Boston: Houghton Mifflin, 1955.

Simons, Robin. *Recyclopedia: Games, Science Equipment and Crafts from Recycled Materials*. Boston: Boston Children's Museum, 1976.

Stecher, Miriam, et al. *Music and Movement Improvisations*. Threshold Early Learning Library, 4. New York: Macmillan, 1972.

Sunderlin, Sylvia, and Nan Grey. *Bits and Pieces*. Washington, D.C.: Association for Childhood Education International, 1967.

Taetzsch, Sandra, and Lyn Taetzsch. *Pre-School Games and Activities*. Belmont, California: Fearon Publishers, 1974.

Young, Percy, and Edward Ardizzone. *Ding Dong Bell*. New York: Dover Publications, Inc., 1957.

"Your Early Education Guide." A notebook reprint from *Grade Teacher*. Darien, Connecticut: CCM Professional Magazines, Inc., Catalogue No. 90972, 1967.

Yurchak, Mary-Jane. *Infant-Toddler Curriculum of the Brookline Early Education Project*. Brookline, Mass: Brookline Early Education Project (BEEP), 1975.

Ziegfeld, Edwin, ed. *Education and Art: A Symposium*. Paris: Unesco, 1953.

SUGGESTED LISTENING

Many of these recordings have been favorites in our classroom. This is not by any means a comprehensive list of all the music it would be possible to play for very young children. You will want to make your own choices. Compositions rather than specific performances have been listed. Excerpting one important section from a larger piece of music isolates it in a way that helps small children understand and enjoy it more easily. Borrow from music libraries wherever possible, and enjoy many fine hours of good listening with your children!

Bach, J.S. *Brandenburg Concerti*
——. Concerto in D. for Two Violins.
——. Sonatas and Partitas for Unaccompanied Violin.
——. Suites for Unaccompanied Cello.
Barber, Samuel. Adagio for Strings.
Bartok, Bela. Concerto for Orchestra.
——. Duos (44) for Two Violins.
Beethoven, Ludwig van. Violin Concerto in D.
——. Concerto in C, for Violin, Cello, and Piano.
——. Sonata No. 5 for Violin and Piano ("The Spring").
——. Symphony No. 6 (The "Pastorale").
Berlioz, Hector. *Symphonie Fantastique.*
Bizet, Georges, *L'Arlesienne,* Suites 1 and 2.
——. *Jeux d'Enfants.*
Brahms, Johannes. Concerto in D for Violin.
——. Concerto in A for Violin and Cello.
——. Sonatas for Violin and Piano.
——. *Symphonies* (Complete).
Britten, Benjamin. *Ceremony of Carols.*
——. *Noye's Fludde.*
——. *Young Person's Guide to the Orchestra.*
Chausson, Ernest. Poeme for Violin and Orchestra.
Corelli, Arcangelo. Concerto Grosso Op. 6. No. 8 ("Christmas").
Debussy, Claude. *Images pour Orchestre.*
——. *Nocturnes.*
——. Quartet in G, Op. 10.
Dohnanyi, Ernst. *Variations on a Nursery Song.*
Dukas, Paul. "The Sorcerer's Apprentice."
Dvorak, Antonin. Concerto for Cello and Orchestra.

——. Quartet No. 12 in F ("The American").

——. *Slavonic Dances.*

——. Symphony No. 9 in E ("From the New World").

Elgar, Edward. *Serenade in E for Strings.*

Falla, Manuel de. "Three-Cornered Hat."

Franck, Cesar. Sonata in A for Violin and Piano.

Grieg, Edvard. *Peer Gynt Suites, Numbers 1 and 2.*

Handel, George Frederic. *Messiah.*

——. *Water Music* (Suite).

Haydn, Franz Joseph. Symphony No. 94 in G ("Surprise").

——. *Toy Symphony.*

Hindemith, Paul. *Symphonic Metamorphosis of Themes by Weber.*

Humperdinck, Engelbert. *Hansel and Gretel* (Selections).

Lalo, Edouard. *Symphonie Espagnole,* for Violin and Orchestra.

Mendelssohn, Felix. Concerto in E for Violin.

——. Octet in E-flat for Strings.

——. Symphony No. 4 in A ("The Italian").

——. Trio No. 1 in D.

Menotti, Gian Carlo. *Amahl and the Night Visitors.*

Mozart, Wolfgang Amadeus. Concerto No. 4 in D, for Violin.

——. Concerto in C, for Flute and Harp.

——. Concerto No. 5 in A, for Violin.

——. Concerto for Piano and Orchestra, No. 21 in C.

——. Overtures.

——. Quintet for Clarinet and Strings.

——. Serenade in G ("Eine Kleine Nachtmusik").

——. Sinfonia Concertante in E-flat, for Violin and Viola.

——. Symphonies Nos. 32, 35, 36, 38, 39, 40, 41.

Prokofiev, Sergei, "Cinderella" (ballet excerpts).

——. Concerti (2) for Violin and Orchestra.

——. *Peter and the Wolf.*

——. *Romeo and Juliet.*

——. Symphony No. 1 in D ("Classical").

Ravel, Maurice. *Ma Mere l'Oye.*

——. Quartet in F.

——. Trio for Violin, Cello, and Piano.

Respighi, Ottorino. *The Birds.*

Rimsky-Korsakov, Nicolai. *Scheherazade.*

——. *Coq d'Or Suite.*

Saint-Saëns, Camille. *Carnival of the Animals.*
———. *Danse Macabre.*
Schubert, Franz. Quintet in A ("The Trout").
———. *Rosamunde: Incidental Music.*
———. *Die Schöne Müllerin.*
———. Trio No. 1, in B-flat (Piano).
Schumann, Robert. *Kinderscenen.*
———. Quintet in E-flat, for Piano and Strings.
———. Symphony No. 1 in B-flat ("Spring").
Sibelius, Jean. Concerto in D for Violin.
———. Symphony No. 2 in D.
Strauss, Richard. *Till Eulenspiegel.*
Stravinsky, Igor. *Firebird Suite.*
———. *Pulcinella Suite.*
Tchaikovsky, Piotr Ilyich. Concerto in D for Violin.
———. *The Nutcracker* (complete ballet).
———. *Swan Lake* (complete ballet).
Vaughan Williams, Ralph. *Fantasia on "Greensleeves".*
Vivaldi, Antonio. *Four Seasons.*
———Concerti for 2 Violins and Orchestra.